Home Refinancing

CASHING IN ON
TODAY'S LOW
INTEREST RATES

Home Refinancing

CASHING IN ON TODAY'S LOW INTEREST RATES

DON DE BAT
EDITED BY THOMAS A. KELLY

CONTEMPORARY
BOOKS, INC.
CHICAGO • NEW YORK

Library of Congress Cataloging-in-Publication Data

DeBat, Don.
Home refinancing.

1. Mortgage loans—United States—Refinancing.
I. TItle.
HG2040.5.U5D42 1986 332.7′22′0973 86-16700
ISBN 0-8092-4891-3 (pbk.)

Published by Contemporary Books, Inc.
180 North Michigan Avenue, Chicago, Illinois 60601
Manufactured in the United States of America
Library of Congress Catalog Card Number: 86-16700
International Standard Book Number: 0-8092-4891-3

Published simultaneously in Canada by Beaverbooks, Ltd.
195 Allstate Parkway, Valleywood Business Park
Markham, Ontario L3R 4T8 Canada

Contents

1
The Rush to Refinance

Interest rates for home loans dipped below 10 percent in 1986 for the first time in nearly eight years. Not surprisingly, this made the idea of refinancing existing high-rate mortgages a topic of coffee klatch and cocktail party chatter in millions of homes from coast to coast.

"Should I refinance now, or wait for rates to go lower?"

"I plan to buy a new house in two years. Is it worth it to refinance?"

"How much will it cost to refinance?"

These were some of the questions asked by American homeowners, who considered refinancing.

In 1986, mortgage lending in the United States soared to an estimated $180 billion, up 63 percent from $110 billion in 1985, and triple the $60 billion in home loans made in 1984, reports the Mortgage Bankers Association of America.

Mortgage lending has changed as well as grown. In 1986 the big difference was that approximately 30 percent to 50 percent of all new loans were refinancing of existing mortgages. Typically, refinancing has accounted for 15 percent to 20 percent of loan activity, according to the association.

When interest charges on fixed-rate mortgages first slipped below 10 percent, Charlie Ferraro, an assistant vice president for mortgage marketing at Bank of New England in Boston said, "We've had craziness here like everyone else. People never thought rates would get down to single digits again. All the recent publicity has sparked a tremendous increase on the refinancing side."

Ronald F. Poe, president of the mortgage bankers group, called 10 percent "the magic number." When the Veterans Administration reduced the top interest rate for VA-guaranteed loans to 9.5 percent from 10 percent in March 1986, it marked the first time VA-backed mortgages were below 10 percent since April 1979. They had hit a peak of 17.5 percent in 1981.

According to Chicago real estate lawyer Marshall J. Moltz, "If you bought a home during the early 1980s at high rates, or purchased one using a short-term balloon loan or other form of creative financing, you should be shopping for long-term fixed-rate financing at a lower rate. Even if you got a loan more recently at 12 percent to 13 percent, it may be to your advantage to refinance."

"For a family that bought a home three or four years ago, refinancing can be just as beneficial to the family budget as getting a $200-a-month-raise," said Sig Anderman, chairman of California-based CompuFund, a national mortgage network.

WHY REFINANCE?

This handbook is designed as a how-to guide for refinancing. It uses a worksheet to lead you step-by-step through the complexities of refinancing. The worksheet takes into account monthly payment, closing costs, and tax and equity factors. It allows you to compare your current loan with a newly refinanced mortgage.

In Chapter 6, easy-to-follow instructions will show you how to calculate all the costs and benefits of refinancing *your* mortgage. Once you finish the calculations, the financial impact of refinancing your mortgage will be clear.

Because interest rates have been on a roller coaster since financial deregulation and restructuring of the mortgage markets in the early 1980s, experts say it is likely that rates for home loans will follow a cycle based on the status of monetary policy, inflation, oil prices, and the economy.

When the cycle is right, smart homeowners should flock to banks, savings and loan associations, mortgage companies, and credit unions to refinance high-rate home loans and reduce their monthly payments. Most recently, the trend has been for borrowers to trade the hefty monthly mortgage payments connected to a loan at 12 percent or 13 percent for 15- or 30-year fixed-rate loans at about 10 percent.

Faced with a sea of rising debts, one couple (we'll call them Jim and Kathy Homeowner) were among thousands of cash-strapped homeowners who learned the budget-saving art of refinancing early in 1986.

"We thought we'd have to sell," said Kathy. The couple's home was a good investment, but new-car payments, higher utility bills, and the cost of raising their two children finally caught up with them.

The Homeowners traded a 15.5 percent, 30-year mortgage for a 10.5 percent, 20-year loan and slashed their monthly housing expenses to $705 from $859. Not only will they be paying less each month, but their equity in the home will grow faster, and they will own the house outright years sooner.

Some borrowers are refinancing to escape the uncertainty of adjustable-rate mortgages (ARMs), especially those without rate limits. Lenders say a large percentage of the recent refinancing volume involves homeowners switching to fixed-rate loans from ARMs. Many of these borrowers were lured to ARMs by the "bargain" of low initial rates.

Even if the recent decline in rates has pushed down interest charges on adjustable mortgages, it may be a good time to lock in a fixed rate on a mortgage and avoid the worry about rising rates, said Richard Peach, vice president for forecasting at the National Association of Realtors. Many homeowners with ARMs have refinanced into fixed-rate mortgages in the belief that rates have virtually hit bottom and payments on an ARM would only get bigger in the next few years.

Moving up to a bigger home when mortgage rates are low is another incentive for refinancing. "Everyone recognizes how lower interest rates have enabled thousands of additional households to qualify for loans to purchase a home, but many homeowners have overlooked the fact that it is quite possible the monthly payments they now are making could enable them to buy a larger, upgraded home through refinancing," notes lender Anderman.

For example, a borrower who in 1982 took out a 30-year fixed-rate loan for $60,000 at 15 percent paid $758.67 a month for principal and interest. When rates fell to 10 percent in 1986, the borrower could have sold the existing home and obtained an $85,000 loan on a bigger house for a smaller monthly payment of $745.94.

Loans taken out at 12 percent or 13 percent can be refinanced with similar—though less dramatic—results. Lower rates also have qualified many more buyers to purchase their first house, allowing borrowers to profit on resales.

Even when mortgage rates are not at bargain levels, homeowners can refinance to free cash that has been locked up as equity. They can then use the cash in various ways, including investing; remodeling; or paying second mortgages, college tuition, or divorce settlements.

THE COSTS OF REFINANCING

Regardless of why you decide to refinance, it's wise to know what you are getting into.

First, you will have to jump through bureaucratic hoops as a lender decides whether your credit history and your home meet its standards. There will be forms to fill out, salary confirmations sent to your employer, and an appraisal made. All this happens only after you have tracked down the best possible loan for your needs.

The costs of refinancing can be high, easily running into thousands of dollars. There also are significant income-tax and equity implications for homeowners who refinance.

Experts provide two rules of thumb in deciding whether to refinance:

Rule 1: The new interest rate must be two to three percentage points lower than your current rate, and you must plan to stay in your home for two or three years.

That's unquestionably true, but what if you can see only two or three years ahead? We have a way to figure it out.

Rule 2: Subtract the available new rate from your current mortgage rate. The difference must be equal to—or greater than—the "points," or closing costs, you will be charged to refinance. One point is equal to 1 percent of the loan amount. Most lenders now are charging two to three points for refinancing.

For example, when Bob and Barbara Bungalow recently refinanced the $70,000 mortage on their home, they cut 2.5 percentage points off their interest rate and reduced the monthly principal and interest payment by $112. But the lender also charged the Bungalows closing costs of 2.5 points, or $1,750.

"The trigger for considering a refinancing is normally that the current mortgage rate should fall at least 2 percent below your existing rate," said mortgage banker Poe. "That just qualified darn near everyone who has taken out a mortgage in the 1980s to consider refinancing."

However, points, a special one-time fee charged by lenders to increase their profits, must be carefully weighed. Total closing fees can rise to between 4 percent and 6 percent of the mortgage amount when the points are added to the application fee, title search and insurance, attorney fees, credit report, appraisal, recording fees, and mortgage insurance.

Both rules of thumb are oversimplifying. To determine whether refinancing makes sense for you, this book goes beyond these simple rules. It uses hard numbers—your numbers—to help you decide. But more about that in Chapter 6.

You'll also find out about the ways to avoid out-of-pocket expenses. Refinance with a new loan large enough to cover the cost of closing. This assumes the property will be appraised at the higher loan amount. But remember, you repay $3.16 over 30 years for every $1 you borrow at 10 percent.

TAX CONSEQUENCES

Homeowners also should consider the tax consequences of refinancing. When computing federal income taxes, you can deduct from income the interest paid on a mortgage. The interest you pay is highest in the early years of the loan, so the deductions also are largest then. If you refinance a high-rate 30-year mortgage with a low rate 15-year loan, you will lose significant tax breaks.

"If you reduce your monthly payments, it is likely that you reduce the interest deductions, and tax write-offs will be less," warns Chicago Certified Public Accountant Frank Pipal.

It is also important to know exactly when the new rate you are applying for will be established. With rates fluctuating daily, a homeowner should determine whether the rate on the day of the application will be the same on the day of closing. Some banks may charge up to a full point extra to lock a homeowner in to a chosen rate before the actual closing.

Lenders also tell mortgage holders to consider how long it will take for lower monthly payments to recoup the fees involved in taking out a new loan. In some cases, it may not be worth it to refinance.

Although individual cases vary because lenders charge differing fees for loans, the savings from refinancing can be substantial. The following chapters will help you decide whether *you* can be one of the many people who are enjoying the benefits of refinancing.

2

The Interest-Rate Roller Coaster

Obviously, the best time to refinance a high-rate home loan is during a period of low interest rates.

However, to understand why mortgage rates dropped below 10 percent in 1986, creating a stampede of refinancing activity and a boom in the housing industry, first you have to understand the movements of interest rates over the past five or six decades.

Mortgage rates have come a long way since the 1920s, when home buyers were required to place a 50 percent down payment and finance the balance with a five-year balloon-payment loan. A balloon is a short-term loan that requires a lump sum payment of the entire principal amount at the end of a specified term, usually 3 to 10 years. Monthly payments on a balloon loan usually are amortized on a 30-year schedule. When many balloon loans "popped," or came due, during the Great Depression of the 1930s, millions of borrowers couldn't afford to pay off the loans and lost their houses.

In 1934, Congress created the Federal Housing Administration (FHA) to encourage home ownership in the United

States. The FHA created the first government-backed long-term home loans that could be paid off in affordable monthly installments.

In those days, home loans had interest rates of 3 percent to 4 percent. It wasn't until the 1950s, when inflation started to heat up, that all interest rates, including those on mortgages, gradually began to climb. By the early 1960s, lenders were charging 6 percent on 30-year mortgages.

THE TIGHT MONEY ERA

After decades of relative stability, mortgage rates began to seesaw in the early 1970s. At the beginning of the decade, mortgage rates were in the 7 percent range. However, recession, the oil crisis, and the "tight money" period of 1973–74 sent rates up to 9 percent. At this time many states still had usury laws that set maximum rates for home loans. During the housing boom of 1975 through 1978, rates again stabilized in the range of 8 percent to 9 percent.

However, deregulation of the banking industry and the recession of 1980–82 sent mortgage rates skyrocketing to an unprecedented 18 percent—when lenders were willing even to make loans.

Many changes happened quickly. Usury laws were wiped out. Deregulation lifted limits on interest rates that lenders could offer depositors. Deregulation also brought such innovations as the adjustable-rate mortgage (ARM), which allows lenders to increase or decrease the interest rate based on movement of key economic indicators, or indexes.

After deregulation, lenders declared that the fixed-rate, long-term mortgage was dead. They said the volatile marketplace made it impossible for them to lock in rates for 20 to 30 years. Instead, they said, mortgage rates would vary with economic conditions.

Soon afterward, economists and lenders said the single-digit mortgage was dead. Forecasters said mortgage rates of nine percent would never be seen again in our lifetime.

REBIRTH OF FIXED-RATE LOANS

In the recovery years of 1983 and 1984, fixed-rate mortgages gradually declined to the range of 12 percent to 14 percent. By 1985, fixed mortgages were down to 11 percent. A wide variety of ARM loans at initial discounted rates of 8 percent to 10 percent also were available.

Deeply discounted single-digit ARMs enjoyed a brief popularity in 1983–85. At one point, lenders boasted that ARMs accounted for half their new loan business. However, the gloomy predictions about fixed-rate mortgages proved to be incorrect.

Early in 1986, borrowers were elated. For the first time in more than seven years, long-term, fixed-rate home loans again were available at 9 percent to 10 percent. Some 70 percent of the home loans originated in 1986 carried fixed rates as refinancing began to gather steam.

What caused interest rates to tumble?

Most economists agree that Reaganomics' curbing of inflation brought down all interest rates, sparking the refinancing boom. After several years of inflation at less than 5 percent a year, even the most cynical observers began to believe that double-digit price increases wouldn't return quickly.

RATES AND OIL PRICES

However, the decline in oil prices also played a major role. In the 1970s, soaring oil prices were blamed for the surge in interest rates. Experts say the subsequent decline in oil prices reinforced the notion of economic stability. Passage by Congress of the Gramm-Rudman Act, which aims to curb deficit spending, also gave a psychological lift to those who doubted that balancing the budget is a real goal of the Reagan administration.

Also, the Federal Reserve Board helped bring interest rates down. The Fed's monetary policy allowed enough money to flow into the system to keep the economy moving, but not enough to create an inflationary condition in which too many dollars chase too few goods.

Because inflation is subdued and appears likely to stay that way, investors and bank depositors are accepting sharply lower interest rates on their money. As a result, financial institutions can afford to reduce mortgage rates while maintaining a high profit margin between the interest they pay out and what they charge.

Lenders also have been freed of some of the risk in making long-term, fixed rate home loans because a strong secondary mortgage market has been created. Today, loan wholesalers, such as the Federal National Mortgage Association, the Federal Home Loan Mortgage Corporation, and the Government National Mortgage Association, package home loans as securities.

Established by Congress to buy FHA loans in 1938 when credit was scarce, FNMA (Fannie Mae), is the largest single investor in residential mortgages. It became a private, for-profit corporation in 1968 and began buying conventional loans in 1970. Acting like a giant savings and loan, Fannie Mae is a mortgage conduit system. It buys mortgages from lenders, packages them into securities and holds them in its portfolio.

GNMA, or Ginnie Mae, was established as an arm of HUD in 1968 to provide secondary-market support for the government's housing programs. It buys FHA and VA mortgages, pools them into securities and then sells them to investors.

FHLMC, nicknamed Freddie Mac, was established in 1970 to provide a secondary market for conventional loans. All of its stock is owned by the Federal Home Loan Bank system and much of its business is with savings and loans. Freddie Mac packages its loans in pools and sells participation certificates to investors.

With stocks and bonds, these securities compete in the open market for investors' dollars, making available to housing much larger amounts of money than could be accumulated from deposits in banks and savings and loan associations. So, lenders need not hold the mortgages they make, and money from home loans is recycled, freeing more funds for borrowers at market rates. Borrowers continue to make payments to the original lender, unaware of any difference.

Although the mortgage market has been relatively stable in recent months, experts say economic factors such as high inflation and expansive monetary policy can bring a return to roller-coaster interest rates.

However, competition created by deregulation of the banking industry, and the development of the home-loan conduit system, means it is likely that American homeowners will have an ample supply of mortgage money in the future.

HISTORY OF FIXED-RATE MORTGAGE INTEREST

Table 2.1 shows long-term effective interest rates charged by savings institutions for conventional loans on new homes in 1965–85.

TABLE 2.1 EFFECTIVE INTEREST RATES, CONVENTIONAL HOME MORTGAGES

Year	*Rate*	*Year*	*Rate*	*Year*	*Rate*
1965	5.81%	1975	9.00	1981	14.70
1970	8.45	1976	9.00	1982	15.14
1971	7.74	1977	9.02	1983	12.66
1972	7.60	1978	9.56	1984	12.37
1973	7.96	1979	10.78	1985	11.58
1974	8.92	1980	12.66		

Source: Compiled by the U.S. League of Savings Institutions from figures gathered by the Federal Home Loan Bank Board.

3
Shopping for the Best Mortgage

Once you decide to refinance, the next step is selecting the right type of mortgage for your pocketbook. Shopping for a home loan today is like taking a trip to the supermarket on the weekend. Lenders have a wide assortment of products to peddle, so it pays to know your way around the mortgage marketplace before you start.

Generally, lenders are eager to handle refinancing because these loans generate new fee income. And lenders consider borrowers who refinance at a lower rate to be better credit risks and less likely to default.

Be prepared to spend some time. When loan rates are low, mortgage makers tend to be very busy. If loan applications are pouring in for refinancing, you might be put on a waiting list for an appointment. Getting an appraisal back can take two or three weeks instead of the usual five days. Heavy volume may cause some lenders to take 60 days—instead of the usual 30 days—to process the loan papers and issue a commitment.

TIPS FOR THE HUNT

Mortgage experts give the following shopping list for families thinking about refinancing their home mortgage.

Where to Start

Begin the mortgage hunt at the institution or mortgage company that financed your current home loan. It could be the best place to refinance because you may be able to eliminate some of the closing costs the second time around. After all, the lender knows whether you make prompt payments, and it previously qualified your income and home for a mortgage. Also most lenders want to keep their loyal customers. However, don't assume your lender has the best deals. Check around. Some lenders charge higher rates because they aren't all that interested in home mortgages.

Don't Be Overanxious

Don't get locked into accepting the first loan you're offered without making certain it's the best available at the time. With the frequent fluctuation of rates these days, no lender has the best deal even half the time.

Shop Around

Although it may be more fun to shop for bargain prices on a videocassette recorder, it can be much more rewarding if you take the time to find a mortgage deal. Get quotations from at least three lending institutions—preferably many more. A few extra phone calls could save you hundreds of dollars.

For example, if you inquire at a bank or S&L around April 15—right after the federal income-tax deadline—you might find the institution loaded with cash from Individual Retirement Account (IRA) deposits. Some S&Ls also have a glut of money from loan repayments sparked by refinancing.

If you find an eager lender, you may be able to negotiate a lower mortgage rate, and there also may be lower point charges. Reducing the interest rate by as little as 0.25 percent can save thousands of dollars over the life of a fixed-rate loan.

Compare More Than Interest Rates

Ask what other charges you will have to pay. These could include points, loan origination fee, application fee, appraisal fee, and many more charges.

Consider Shorter Mortgages

Don't be afraid of shorter-term loans. At the lower rates available in 1986, thousands of borrowers took on shorter-term loans. Some homeowners opted for 15-year fixed-rate mortgages and ended up with lower payments and faster equity build-up than on their old 30-year loans.

For example, the monthly payment on a 30-year mortgage of $50,000 at 13 percent is $553.10. If you refinance with a 15-year loan at 10 percent, the monthly payment will be $537.31.

Trading a 30-year loan for a 15-year loan also can eliminate 10 to 14 years of payments, depending on how long you had the previous loan. The savings on interest could amount to tens of thousands of dollars, and the gain in equity will be substantial.

On a $50,000 loan at 10 percent for 15 years, you would owe $40,650 after five years. Had you chosen a 30-year loan at 10 percent, you would owe $48,300 after five years.

The difference is even more dramatic after 15 years. While for the 15-year loan you would be holding a mortgage-burning party, on the 30-year mortgage you'd still owe $40,850. (To figure the savings on your loan amount, see the mortgage progress chart on pages 107–10 in the Appendix.)

Ask Questions

It also pays to inquire about different loan programs because lenders now are offering so many new types of mortgage instruments. The programs vary from one institution to another. If a bank or S&L says it will refinance using only an adjustable-rate mortgage, and you don't want that, go elsewhere.

Beware of Rate Fluctuations

It is important to ask exactly when the new rate you are applying for will be established. With rates fluctuating daily, a homeowner should determine if the new contract rate will be the one available on the day of application, or the one available on the day of the actual closing. Find out if the institution is one that charges up to a full point extra if a homeowner wants to be locked in to a chosen rate before the actual closing.

Check Into Uncle Sam's Programs

Don't forget government-backed loan programs. Ask the local Federal Housing Administration office if your house is eligible for an FHA-insured loan. Eligibilty depends on a maximum price level by geographic region. For example, in the Chicago area the maximum FHA-loan amount is $87,250, in New York; it's $90,000; and in San Francisco it's $90,000. If you or your spouse served in the military, you may be eligible for a no-money-down, Veterans Administration-guaranteed loan.

Don't Wait Forever

In every interest-rate cycle, some borrowers want to wait until rates hit bottom. Don't worry about getting the absolutely lowest rate. Experts say borrowers should cut their refinancing deal when rates are in the trough of the cycle—not when they start to head up.

When even Wall Street's wizards can't figure how low rates will go, the best advice is to take a deal that makes financial sense. Your rate may not be absolutely lowest, but you will be thousands of dollars ahead of where you would be stuck if you didn't refinance.

Refinancing Isn't for Everyone

Don't refinance if you are planning to move in three years or less. Generally, it takes that long for lower payments to make up for refinancing fees. But be realistic—many Americans stay in their "starter" houses much longer than they expect. If you know you will move fairly soon, the only way refinancing will pay off is if you take out an assumable mortgage, such as an FHA or VA loan. When you sell your house, the buyer can take over the mortgage payments. This can make your house especially attractive if the going rate then is higher than the rate on your mortgage.

Refinancing Older Mortgages

Some homeowners choose to refinance older mortgages to use their equity for major home improvements, such as adding a room or remodeling. Experts say you should think twice about refinancing if you've had a 30-year mortgage for more than 15 years. The interest rate is a single-digit bargain and payments tend to be low. The majority of your monthly payment is going toward paying off your mortgage balance, and equity is building fast.

If your mortgage is more than 10 years old, your rate is probably lower than anything available today. Leave well enough alone. An alternative source for tapping that built-up equity might be a second mortgage, a home improvement loan, or a home-equity loan.

POPULAR LOAN OPTIONS

Mortgage lenders have more types of loans to offer than ever before, but many of them may not be for you. Here are details on some of the most popular options for refinancing loans available at banks, savings and loans associations, and mortgage companies:

Conventional Fixed-Rate Loans

Most conventional fixed-rate loans have terms of 15 years or 30 years. Although fixed-rate loans have higher initial interest charges than adjustable-rate mortgages, these "old-fashioned" loans let the borrower know the exact amount of the home-loan payments for the next 180 or 360 months. With adjustable-rate loans, payments can rise and fall with market conditions, leaving a homeowner worrying what the monthly housing expense will be.

Table 3.1 shows the monthly principal and interest payments for a 30-year and a 15-year fixed-rate mortgage for $50,000.

TABLE 3.1 MONTHLY PAYMENTS OF PRINCIPAL AND INTEREST (FIXED-RATE LOAN FOR $50,000)

Interest Rate	*15-Year Loan*	*30-Year Loan*
8.0%	$477.83	$366.89
8.5	492.37	384.46
9.0	507.14	402.08
9.5	522.12	420.43
10.0	537.31	438.79
10.5	552.70	457.37
11.0	568.30	476.17
11.5	584.10	495.15
12.0	600.09	514.31
12.5	616.27	533.63
13.0	632.63	553.10
13.5	649.16	572.71
14.0	665.88	592.44
14.5	682.76	612.28
15.0	699.80	632.23

Because the monthly payments are lower, 30-year fixed-rate loans are most popular with young, middle-income families that are trying to keep home expenses to a minimum. You'll pay more interest on a 30-year loan than on a

15-year loan, but this is offset somewhat by the advantage of bigger tax deductions for mortgage interest.

Payments are higher on a 15-year mortgage, but interest rates and points tend to be slightly less than for the 30-year loan. Also, you'll build up equity and pay off the loan faster. Middle-age homeowners prefer to refinance with a 15-year loan because they have higher income and want their house to be paid off before retirement.

Also, ambitious young people who want to be quickly rid of a mortgage prefer the 15-year loan. Even for those who plan to stay in their home for a few years, it is a good choice for making equity increase rapidly. (See the loan progress charts on pages 107–10 in the Appendix.)

Government-Backed Loans

Fixed-rate FHA-insured and VA-guaranteed loans are popular mortgages for refinancing. Although the money for these 15-year and 30-year mortgages usually comes from mortgage bankers, these loans are backed by Uncle Sam. They are particularly attractive because of low down-payment requirements and affordable interest rates. In addition, government-backed loans are fully assumable with no prepayment penalties. Disadvantages include red tape and delay in applying and the possibility of substantial closing fees, or points.

Adjustable-Rate Mortgages

Most banks and S&Ls would prefer borrowers to choose ARMs because the flexible rate protects the institution in times of inflation and recession. Instead of being locked into fixed-rate obligations—as many S&Ls and banks were in the early 1980s—the financial institution can pass along rate increases allowed under terms of the loan and maintain its profit margin.

As a bank or savings and loan pays higher interest rates to savers, ARM borrowers pay the freight. ARM loans often are indexed to the lender's cost-of-funds, so that in times of recession and high interest rates a bank or savings and loan isn't locked into a low-yield, fixed-rate mortgage portfolio.

Here's how an ARM works: Lenders adjust the interest rate on the loan at regular intervals—usually every one, three, or five years—based on an index. Then they add a profit margin to compute the new rate. Typical indexes include the one-year Treasury Bill Index, an average of U.S. securities yields, or the Federal Home Loan Bank Board's monthly Cost of Funds Index, which charts the average rates paid by federally chartered S&Ls to savers and other lenders.

ARMs got a bad reputation when rates were high and they were the only type of financing many people could afford. More recently, however, consumer protection was added to ARMs in the form of interest rate and payment "caps." Even so, the amount of the monthly check the borrower sends the lender can change annually or every three or five years. That doesn't sit well with many borrowers.

If you are planning to move to another house in two or three years, a bargain-rate ARM, say at 8.5 percent in the first year, might be a useful refinancing tool. For example, if the loan has a 2 percent annual cap, the rate can't rise to more than 10.5 percent at the beginning of the second year, regardless of how high the index shoots up.

Other Alternatives

There also are other financing alternatives, such as graduated-payment loans, 3-year to 10-year balloon loans, and creative financing options that are geared to very specific market segments or economic conditions. These financing methods traditionally are not popular when fixed-rate mortgages are available at low interest rates.

HOW TO SPEED UP AN APPROVAL

During this nationwide refinancing craze, lenders can be buried under a mountain of paperwork. With thousands of applications to process, lenders can take 60 days or longer.

"Homeowners can help speed loan approval by carefully collecting the pertinent financial data and making sure the loan officer gets it quickly," said mortgage analyst Gary S. Meyers, president of Chicago-based Gary S. Meyers & Associates. "Borrowers who refinance with the same lender will not have to provide as much data as those who go to a new lender."

Here are some tips and a list of documents and financial information you'll need to apply for a refinance:

- *Checkbook.* Bring your checkbook. When you first apply, most institutions will charge about $250 to process a loan application. They often won't start the wheels moving until it's paid.
- *Credit report.* Before you apply for a loan, get a copy of your credit record by contacting a credit reporting company in your area. It is well worth the $40 fee to find out if there are any surprises or mistakes listed in your credit background before talking to a loan officer. It's also a good idea for a borrower to go to a reputable credit reporting agency in advance and hire it to do the credit check. While you are hunting for a lender, the credit work will be under way. When you apply for the loan, you can notify the lender that the report is completed. If you don't know of such an agency in your area, ask potential lenders which agency they use. Then contact the agency directly.
- *Employment verification.* You will be asked to sign a verification form that will be sent to your employer. Know the name of a person at your company who verifies employment and alert this person that an inquiry is coming. If you've been with your current company for less than two years, you should have the same information and personnel contact with your former employer.
- *Proof of income.* You will need your federal income-tax returns for the past two years, especially if you are self-employed. When quoting current or expected income, be sure to include any commissions, bonuses, or regular overtime pay. Child support and alimony also should be shown, whether you give it or get it.

- *Bank accounts.* Provide account or certificate numbers for your checking and savings accounts, as well as the addresses of the financial institutions. You also should list any stock or bond holdings, because they would increase your financial standing in the lender's eyes. Find out where the institutions give out credit information. It may be the main office, not the branch office where you bank.
- *Credit cards.* Give account numbers of all your major credit cards. Make sure all accounts are current, and clean up any delinquencies before you apply for the loan.
- *Outstanding loans.* The account number and addresses of all lenders must be provided. This includes real estate and personal loans.
- *Previous loans.* If you've paid off other loans, including student loans, list them and the lenders. Credit companies often lack the information and don't report loans that are paid off. Make sure you get credit for having paid off loans.
- *Copies of all documents.* When supplying a lender with information, do not send original documents—copies are acceptable. Any papers mailed should be sent with a return-receipt request. To avoid delays, address the papers to a specific person at the lending institution.
- *Questionable debts.* If you have any questionable debts, or there are any special circumstances regarding your credit background, tell the loan officer. Anything out of the ordinary that shows up on your credit report must be explained. Make it as easy as possible for a busy loan officer to approve your mortgage.

WHAT CAN YOU AFFORD

To help protect themselves—and the borrower—financial institutions across the nation have tightened their credit requirements and limited the total debt borrowers are allowed to carry and still receive loan approval.

The limits recently have been changed to 28 percent of *gross* income for mortgage payments and 36 percent for total debt (including credit cards and auto loans, for example).

The limits had been 33 percent for mortgage payments and 38 percent for total debt.

This means if your gross income is $2,000 per month, the highest monthly mortgage payment you may qualify for is $560 per month. Your total monthly debt payment cannot exceed $720 per month.

It takes time for a borrower to carefully prepare all of the information the lender needs to approve his or her mortgage application. But the extra effort should pay off in faster loan approval. Remember: when interest rates and points are fluctuating daily, faster approval could save you money.

4
The Costs of Refinancing

At first glance, the downside risk of refinancing your mortgage appears to be slight. However, substantial costs in time and money are involved. Chapter 3 described the time and effort of shopping for a loan and speeding along its processing. This chapter will discuss the financial costs of refinancing a mortgage.

"There are a number of transaction costs that homeowners should be aware of when judging the value of refinancing," said Warren Lasko, executive vice president of the Mortgage Bankers Association of America.

When you refinance, you have to go through closing again, so there will be expenses that may offset the savings from a lower interest rate. You do not have to pay transfer taxes again, but you will have to buy some of the same appraisal, credit, and title reports and pay lawyers' fees.

A homeowner who now has a 30-year, fixed-rate mortgage for $65,000 at 13 percent is paying $719.03 a month for principal and interest. Refinancing the entire amount at 10 percent would cut payments to $570.43, a savings of $148.60 a month.

POINTS: THE MAJOR COST

Closing costs, including points, must be carefully weighed. Most lenders now are charging two to three points for refinancing. On government-insured loans, these fees can run as much as five points, or 5 percent of the mortgage amount. In some cases, a lender may waive or reduce points if a borrower is a good customer of the institution.

Before a homeowner leaps into refinancing to "save" $100 to $200 a month on his or her mortgage payment, the family's plans about staying in the house must be examined.

On that $65,000 refinance, for example, let's assume that the lender charged three points (each point represents a $650 charge) and $400 in other fees at closing. The cost of refinancing would total $2,350. But with the reduced monthly payment of $148.60, the homeowner would save $2,377.60 over the next 16 months. (Clearly, this simple analysis does not take into consideration tax factors.)

Often, however, total closing costs are much higher. Total closing fees can amount to between 4 percent and 6 percent of the mortgage amount, according to the Mortgage Bankers Association of America.

Why must you pay so much to refinance a loan you took out only a year or two ago? Lenders say refinancing really is taking out a new mortgage, and borrowers have to pay the freight of originating the loan.

But consumer advocates say it costs the lender only $300 to $500 to put a new mortgage on the books. And that's if you refinance with a different lender, borrow more money, or shorten the term of your loan. If you just want to renegotiate a lower rate with the same lender for the outstanding balance of the loan, and not extend or shorten the term, the lender's costs may only be $100.

Mortgage fees, like the price of a new car, are negotiable. They tend to be substantially higher than the actual cost of doing the work because lenders are out to make a profit and charge what the market will bear. When rates are low and refinancing acitivity is high, some lenders cash in.

On points, for example, it is not uncommon for one mortgage company to charge 2 percent of the loan amount, while another lender will ask four points for a mortgage at the same rate.

Lenders also are willing to make a tradeoff between points and the interest rate. For example, if the market rate is 10 percent, but a borrower is determined to lock in a mortgage at 9.75 percent, the lender may agree to the lower rate, but charge an extra point or two in upfront fees.

Also, banks and S&Ls place high value on keeping their customers. So it is not uncommon for some institutions to charge lower fees and points to prevent borrowers from moving their business elsewhere. If you decide to refinance with your original lender, you may be able to negotiate a reduction of points or a waiver of title search, application fee, credit check, or other fees.

OTHER CLOSING COSTS

Just what are these fees besides points? Among the non–tax deductible expenses you may have to pay when refinancing a home loan are: title search, title exam insurance, application fee, credit report, real estate lawyer fees, reappraisal fee, prepayment penalty, loan origination fee, recording taxes, and mortgage insurance. On FHA loans, another fee—which *is* tax deductible—is interest in arrears.

Title Search and Insurance Fees

The title policy, usually issued by a title insurance company, assures payment to any claimant in case of discrepancies in the property's title. If the refinancing lender goes through the same title company, a reissue of an existing policy can save as much as 75 percent of the fees. The search generally costs $15 to $60.

Cost for a new title policy depends on the loan amount, but expect to pay about $400. However, you could pay as little as $100 by using the same title company if a "substitution loan rate" policy can be issued rather than a new owner's policy.

Application Fee

Lenders usually charge a fee for processing the loan application. This fee may cover other costs, including credit check and appraisal. Ask a lender what the application fee covers. Cost: About $250.

Credit Report

Sometimes this is included in the loan application fee. If you refinance at the lending institution that holds the original mortgage, this fee may be waived. If you refinance at a different lender, the new lender will order a report on your credit history. Cost: $40 to $50.

Real Estate Lawyer Fees

As in all real estate transactions, you should hire your own lawyer. You are making a contract to pay tens of thousands of dollars, so expert advice is recommended.

"A refinancing can be confusing, depending on the circumstances of the deal," said Chicago real estate lawyer Marshall J. Moltz. "Generally the fee is much less on a refinance if you go to the same lawyer who handled the original closing." Cost: $150 to $400, depending on the complexity of the closing.

Reappraisal Fee

This is an estimate of the value of your property. The charge covers the cost of making sure your house is worth enough to justify your loan amount. Sometimes this is included in the application fee. Cost: $75 to $150.

Prepayment Penalty

Your existing mortgage may have a prepayment penalty. Check your loan contract. Although the practice of charging money for early payment of the old mortgage varies, a ceiling of 1 to 2 percent of the outstanding principal usually is placed on the penalty. It could run $500 to $1,000 on a $50,000 loan. Prepayment penalties are forbidden on all FHA-insured and VA-guaranteed loans.

Loan Origination Fee

This usually is a percentage of the loan amount. It's like a point in every way but one; it's not tax-deductible. Cost: Usually 1 percent of the loan amount. On a $50,000 loan it would run $500.

Survey

The survey shows the lengths and directions of the boundary lines of the property surveyed and the location of all buildings and other improvements. Lenders usually require a current survey to ensure there are no encroachments on the property that would hamper a future sale. Cost: $75 to $150.

Document Preparation

All that paper shuffling costs money. So do the notary services. Cost: Expect to pay about $50.

Recording Fees

When the new mortgage is drafted, it must be recorded at the county or township clerk's office where the property is located. Cost: $25 to $35.

Interest in Arrears

When an FHA loan is refinanced, lenders can charge interest in arrears, which in effect is a prepayment penalty. If a borrower prepays an FHA loan, the lender has the right to insist on receiving the prepayment on the first of the month. If the refinanced loan closes after the first of the month, the lender can charge an additional 30 days interest in arrears.

Private Mortgage Insurance

Depending on the amount of equity you have in your house, another expense of refinancing can be private mortgage insurance. PMI is an insurance policy that protects the lender from loss in the event of a foreclosure. The consumer pays for it, and lenders require it on loans with low down payments. Most lenders charge PMI on all loans with down payments of less than 20 percent.

With a down payment or equity of 5 percent, the initial insurance premium is 1.25 percent of the loan amount. So, if you refinanced a $50,000 loan, but currently have less than 20 percent equity in the property, you would have to pay a private mortgage insurance premium of $625 at closing. Each subsequent year, PMI would be charged at 0.44 percent of the unpaid balance of the loan.

If you have equity of 10 percent in the property, and refinance a $50,000 loan, the initial insurance premium at closing is 0.5 percent of the loan amount, or $250. Each subsequent year, PMI is charged at 0.34 percent of the unpaid balance.

With equity of 15 percent in your home, the initial premium is charged at 0.35 percent of the loan amount. So, on a $50,000 refinancing, the premium due at closing would be $175. Each year, PMI is charged at 0.34 percent of the loan amount. In Texas and Pennsylvania slightly higher renewal premium percentages are used. Check with local lenders.

PMI usually is discontinued when the outstanding principal of the loan drops below 80 percent.

HOW TO AVOID SOME OF THOSE FEES

As mentioned previously, check with your original lender before signing up for the lowest-rate mortgage in town. It is likely that costs to refinance will be less because title search, title insurance, and credit report may still be up to date.

Generally, lenders are eager to handle a refinancing because this generates new fee income. And borrowers who refinance at a lower rate usually are better credit risks because the monthly payments are less, the mortgage term is shorter, or both.

To compare the range of fees lenders charge, use the handy chart in Table 4.1. Simply go down the list with a lender so you know exactly what you will have to pay.

If you don't have the cash to pay all these closing costs, don't give up. You could refinance with a loan large enough to cover the cost. Of course, your home would have to be

TABLE 4.1 REFINANCING FEES

Title Search	\$15–\$60
Title Insurance	\$100–\$400
Credit Report	\$0–\$50
Lawyer Fee	\$150–\$400
Reappraisal Fee	\$75–\$300
Loan Origination Fee	\$0–\$500
Prepayment Penalty	\$0–\$1,000
Application Fee	\$250
Recording Taxes	\$25–\$35
Mortgage Insurance	\$0–\$500
Survey	\$75–\$150
Document Preparation	\$0–\$50
Other Fees	\$0–\$100

appraised at enough to cover the higher loan amount, or you would have to give up some of your equity.

If the appraised value is there, lenders usually will add the refinancing charges to the new loan, as long as it doesn't exceed 85 percent of a home's value for a government-insured loan, or 90 percent for a conventional loan.

TALLY THE COSTS

Before you decide to go ahead with refinancing, it's a good idea to do a final tally of the costs. The worksheet in Chapter 6 will help you determine whether refinancing pays. But first, study Table 4.1, which outlines the range of nondeductible fees on a typical \$50,000 refinancing. Points are excluded from the table because they are tax deductible.

5
The Implications of Refinancing

Owning a home produces such important tax breaks that Congress tiptoes in making any changes. Real estate investors say tax advantages may be the biggest financial incentive to buy real estate. Of course, the satisfaction of home ownership, the potential for appreciation, and the locking-in of monthly home costs also figure in.

DEDUCTIBLE EXPENSES

Deductions for mortgage interest and property taxes account for billions of dollars in tax savings each year. Interest paid on a mortgage is deductible from income when computing federal income taxes.

The interest you pay is highest in the early years of the loan, so the deductions also are largest then. If you refinance a high-rate 30-year mortgage with a low-rate 30-year loan, you will lose significant tax breaks. The impact is even more dramatic if you switch to a low-rate 15-year mortgage.

Put simply, the lower the rate on your loan, the smaller the interest deduction you can claim. But don't be discouraged by this. Remember, a homeowner in the 38 percent tax bracket reduces taxes by only $38 for every $100 in annual mortgage interest paid.

DEDUCTING POINTS

The second important impact on taxes involves the costs you pay at closing. The only costs that are deductible are any interest in arrears that you pay (on an FHA loan) and the points you pay to close. Interest in arrears is deductible in the year in which you pay it.

Until May of 1986, the Internal Revenue Service (IRS) made no decision on how individual taxpayers should treat refinance points on their federal income tax returns.

Accountants and lawyers often advised borrowers to deduct the entire cost of points from their taxable income in the year it was paid. Thus, a borrower who refinanced a $50,000 mortgage for 30 years and paid points of 3 percent of the loan amount could claim a $1,500 deduction.

Then, the IRS dropped a bombshell, saying that homeowners cannot immediately deduct the points lenders charge when refinancing a mortgage. The IRS said it interprets the law to mean that points attributed to refinancing must be spread over the life of the loan. It said such points go to repay existing debt, not to buy or improve a home.

Not only is this a bookkeeping nightmare for the homeowner, but it provides tax relief in tiny doses over a long period of time, instead of a large helping on this year's taxes.

Under the new decision, the borrower who paid $1,500 in points on the $50,000 refinancing would be allowed only to deduct $50 each year for the 30 years of the loan. However, if the borrower sells his house before the mortgage is paid off—and then pays off the loan—the remainder of the points fee would be deductible in the year of the sale and the repayment of the mortgage.

Because the IRS said its interpretation would be retroactive, accountants said they fear thousands of taxpayers who took deductions for refinance points will be audited and forced to recompute taxes for 1985 and prior years.

The IRS "came out with the answer people really didn't want to hear," said Jim Schlesser, an accountant and tax specialist for the Chicago office of Touche Ross & Co. Accountants and lawyers predicted that Congress will feel pressure from angry homeowners who refinanced expecting that they could deduct their points. It's not clear whether this pressure will be enough to force Congress to address refinancing points.

Existing law lets borrowers deduct points from taxable income the year they are paid if a loan is for the "purchase or improvement" of a primary residence.

"I think the IRS made the correct ruling based on the wording of the law," said Chicago accountant and attorney John Ahern. The law makes no mention of refinancing mortgages to take advantage of lower interest rates.

However, according to the IRS decision, if part of the refinance money is used for remodeling, the points for that portion of the loan would be deductible.

For example, if $25,000 of the $50,000 loan was used to build a room addition, you could deduct half the points—or $750— in 1986. The balance would have to be deducted over the life of the loan at a rate of $25 a year.

On the other hand, some accountants, such as Frank Pipal of Chicago, recommend that taxpayers deduct the entire amount of the points in the year they are paid. Points, Pipal said, are merely a charge to the consumer for borrowing money.

Because the law does not address the issue of refinancing, these accountants contend that regardless of the IRS decision the usual rules for individual taxpayers should be followed.

"Taxpayers should be able to deduct the entire amount of points charges they pay in the year they are paid. That's because a taxpayer declares all income and expenses in the year earned or paid out," Pipal said.

This is an aggressive approach, but Pipal suggests giving it a try. At worst, the IRS can audit the taxpayer and make him pay on the disallowed points and interest on the tax.

With the ruling, Pipal said the IRS is trying to treat

taxpayers like businesses, which have to spread all financing costs over the life of a loan.

If, however, a taxpayer adds the points to the loan amount, he has no choice but to spread the point charge over the life of the loan.

AN ILLUSTRATION

To illustrate the tax impact of refinancing, let's take a look at an example of one couple who refinanced.

Bob and Barbara Bungalow have a taxable income of $55,000 a year and are carrying a $70,000 mortgage at 13 percent interest for 15 years. Let's suppose they refinance with a 10.5 percent mortgage for the same loan amount and term. Their financial situation would change in several ways:

- *Monthly payments*—Their monthly mortgage payment would drop to $774 from $886, a savings of $112 a month.
- *Interest payments*—On their old loan at 13 percent, the couple would have paid $17,780 in interest over the next two years. However, if they refinance at 10.5 percent, they will pay only $14,280 in interest over the next two years—a reduction of $3,500.
- *Lost Tax Benefits*—The couple's taxable income put them in the 38 percent tax bracket. With $3,500 less in interest deductions, the Bungalow's would lose $1,330 in income-tax benefits:

  $3,500 × 0.38 = $1,330
- *Tax Deduction for Points*—On the other hand, the couple paid points of 2.5 percent of the loan amount or $1,750:

  $70,000 × 0.025 = $1,750

The Bungalows would be able to deduct the $1,750 cost of points over the 15-year life of their refinanced mortgage. In the first two years, therefore, they could deduct $233.33 from their taxable income. In their 38 percent tax bracket, their tax liability would be reduced by $88.67.

$1,750 × 2 divided by 15 × 0.38 = $88.67

So, the $88.67 in tax savings eases the pain a bit on April 15. While the number crunching may seem mind-boggling at first, it sheds some light on the tax implications of refinancing. And remember: *Does it make sense to pay out an extra $100 in interest just to reduce your taxes by $38?*

EQUITY IMPLICATIONS

Despite the loss in tax benefits caused by refinancing, there are other advantages, in addition to cutting your monthly payments. Any time the rate on a loan is lowered, equity in your home builds up much faster. Any time the length of a loan is lowered, equity builds faster. Faster equity buildup is especially important to homeowners who will use their equity to move up to a larger home or who wish to free themselves from mortgage payments quickly.

If you carry less debt, you also have more credit and potentially more cash to spend on a new car, a family vacation, or home improvements.

6

Introduction to the Refinancing Worksheet

Rules of thumb can be useful, but when they affect you and your wallet, it pays to look beyond the generalizations for some specifics.

So it is with the rule that says you should refinance if you can cut at least two percentage points off your rate and you plan to stay in the house two to three years. Or the rule that says the decrease in your rate should equal the number of points you have to pay.

In many cases, those rules of thumb don't give you the whole story. That's because there are tax and equity considerations. Furthermore, lower monthly payments don't always guarantee a better deal, especially if you have paid substantial fees to refinance.

What if you can cut only 1.5 percentage points off the rate? Or what about switching from a 30-year loan to a 15-year loan? There is no simple formula for deciding, but this chapter will lead you through a step-by-step worksheet that lets you see how refinancing *your* mortgage will work out.

You'll know if you'll be ahead or behind after two years—and by how much. Two years was chosen because most people can predict whether they'll be in a home that long. After that, it becomes less certain.

GETTING READY

Before you start plugging in numbers, you need to obtain the following information:

1. Find out the current rate and principal amount of your mortgage.
2. Check around with lenders for the best rate with the fewest fees and points.
3. Ask the lender what closing costs are charged.
4. Make a rough guess of what your taxable income will be for this year. The tax brackets used in this book reflect 1986's rates.

Now, sharpen your pencil, check the batteries in the calculator, and you're ready to start. This worksheet is no harder than an income-tax form—and you won't end up owing the government money.

To make calculations easier, the interest rates have been rounded to the nearest half-percent (pick the one closest to yours), and interest and equity are figured during the first and second years of the loan. (Even if your current loan is in years three and four, the numbers are similar.) As mentioned earlier, it's unlikely that you would want to refinance if your loan is more than six years old—unless you are trying to free some of your home's equity.

To keep this comparison reasonably simple, we assumed no taxes on savings invested or foregone. This simplification won't substantially affect the result. Also, no inflation factor was added, because inflation has slowed to a crawl.

The May, 1986, IRS decision delaying the deduction of the full point expense means that it will take longer to recoup the initial expenses of refinancing than if you could deduct the entire amount in the year of closing.

Once you've finished the calculations, your choice should be clear. If the bottom line (line (21) of the worksheet) is positive, your refinance will pay off within two years. That means it makes excellent financial sense.

If the bottom line is within a few hundred dollars of breaking even after two years, you should go ahead and refinance. Even if you move after two years, you can deduct the remainder of the points expense if you pay off the mortgage then.

If the bottom line is negative by $1,000 or more, think very carefully about refinancing. If you are refinancing a fixed-rate, long-term loan, do it only if you intend to stay in the house at least three or four years.

If you are changing from a balloon loan to a fixed-rate loan, go ahead and do it. And if you are trading in an adjustable-rate mortgage for a fixed-rate for peace of mind, you probably should go ahead. The rates you can lock in today are a bargain compared to those offered for an ARM any time between 1980 and 1985.

As usual, it can pay to shop around. To compare refinancing packages, repeat the calculations using the appropriate figures for each package. You'll find extra worksheets in the Appendix at the back of the book.

FIGURING THE COSTS OF REFINANCING

The best way to understand how refinancing can benefit you is by taking a step-by-step journey through a worksheet designed to calculate the costs and benefits of refinancing.

The worksheet will show you how to compute the costs of paying your old mortgage and compare them with a new loan. You'll compare interest paid on both loans, cash monthly payments on each, and the built-up equity with each.

The worksheet shows the costs and benefits of refinancing after all the variables are compiled.

Nondeductible Costs

Let's start with nondeductible refinancing costs. To figure nondeductible costs, write in all lender, lawyer, and tax fees except points and interest in arrears. Add these costs and enter the total on line (1).

Title Search	$_______
Title Insurance	_______
Credit Report	_______
Lawyer Fee	_______
Reappraisal Fee	_______
Loan Origination Fee	_______
Prepayment Penalty	_______
Application Fee	_______
Recording Taxes	_______
Mortgage Insurance	_______
Other Fees: __________	_______
Total Nondeductible Fees	$_______

Tax-Deductible Costs

Another benefit of refinancing is tax deductibility of a major chunk of the expenses—the points, or extra loan fees lenders usually charge to increase their yield on the loan. Also, for government-backed loans, interest in arrears is required at closing. The vast majority of this is tax-deductible interest.

To figure points, write in the loan amount in thousands. For example, for a $50,000 loan, write in 50. Multiply by the number of points charged and multiply the result by 10. On line (2a), enter the amount you computed.

Total Point Fee:

Loan amount (thousands)		Points charged					
____________	×	____________	× 10	=	$______		(2a)
Interest in Arrears (for FHA borrowers)					$______		(2b)

COMPARING COSTS OF TWO LOANS

Before you start this part of the worksheet, write down the interest rate on your current loan (rounded to the nearest 0.5 percent) and the rate available on a refinanced loan. Also, write down the amount of the loan in thousands of dollars. (For example, if your loan amount is $50,000, write 50). Finally, write down your family's estimated taxable income for this year.

Old rate: ______ New rate: ______

Loan amount (thousands): ______ Estimated annual income: ______

Interest Paid for First Two Years

To figure the total interest paid in the first two years, multiply the loan amount (in thousands) by the interest from Table 6.1. Table 6.1 shows the total interest paid over the first two years for each thousand dollars borrowed. To use this

TABLE 6.1 INTEREST PAID PER $1,000 AFTER TWO YEARS

Interest Rate	*15-Year Loan*	*30-Year Loan*
8.0%	$154	$159
8.5	164	169
9.0	175	179
9.5	185	189
10.0	194	199
10.5	204	209
11.0	214	219
11.5	225	229
12.0	234	239
12.5	244	249
13.0	254	260
13.5	265	269
14.0	275	279
14.5	285	290
15.0	294	300

table, find the rate closest to the current (old) mortgage rate and look across to the number corresponding to a 15-year or 30-year term, whichever is applicable. Then do the same for the new loan, using the rate quoted by the lender.

For example, the first two years' interest on a currently held 13 percent, 15-year loan would be $254. The two-year cost of a new 10.5 percent, 15-year loan would be $204. Pick the rate closest to yours.

Multiply the loan amount in thousands by the two-year interest cost per thousand to find the total interest for the first two years. Then enter the result for the current loan on line (3). Enter the result for the new loan on line (4). To figure the difference, subtract line (4) from line (3). Enter the difference on line (5).

Two Years' Interest on Old Loan:

Loan amount (thousands)		Interest (from Table 6.1)		
____________	×	____________	=	$________

Two Years' Interest on New Loan:

Loan amount Interest

__________ × __________ = ________ (4)

Difference:

Line (3) — Line (4) $________ (5)

Monthly Payments

Next figure the monthly payments for the current and new mortgages. Multiply the loan amount (in thousands) by the cost per thousand dollars. You get this cost from Table 6.2. Enter the monthly payment for the current loan on line (6). Enter the monthly payment for the new loan on line (7).

Now find the difference between the monthly payments. Subtract line (7) from line (6). Enter the difference on line (8).

TABLE 6.2 MONTHLY PAYMENT PER THOUSAND DOLLARS BORROWED

Interest Rate	*15-Year Loan*	*30-Year Loan*
8.0%	$9.56	$7.34
8.5	9.85	7.69
9.0	10.15	8.05
9.5	10.45	8.41
10.0	10.75	8.78
10.5	11.06	9.15
11.0	11.37	9.53
11.5	11.69	9.91
12.0	12.01	10.29
12.5	12.33	10.68
13.0	12.66	11.07
13.5	12.99	11.46
14.0	13.32	11.85
14.5	13.66	12.25
15.0	14.00	12.65

Monthly Payment for Old Loan:

Loan amount (thousands)		Cost per 1,000 (Table 6.2)			
________	×	________	=	$________	(6)

Monthly Payment for New Loan:

Loan amount		Cost per 1,000			
________	×	________	=	________	(7)

Difference:

Line (6) − Line (7) $________ (8)

Equity Buildup After Two Years

Now you are ready to compare how your equity grows under your current mortgage with equity buildup under the new mortgage. This part of the worksheet considers equity buildup after two years. To figure the amount of equity built up, multiply the loan amount (in thousands) by the equity per thousand from Table 6.3.

On line (9), enter the amount of equity built up under the current loan. On line (10), enter the two-year equity buildup

TABLE 6.3 EQUITY EARNED PER $1,000 AFTER TWO YEARS

Interest Rate	*15-Year Loan*	*30-Year Loan*
8.0%	$75	$17
8.5	72	16
9.0	69	14
9.5	66	13
10.0	64	12
10.5	61	11
11.0	59	10
11.5	56	9
12.0	54	8
12.5	52	7
13.0	50	6
13.5	47	6
14.0	45	5
14.5	43	4
15.0	42	4

with the new loan. Now compute the difference; subtract line (9) from line (10). Enter the difference on line (11).

Two Years' Equity with Old Loan:

Loan amount (thousands)		Equity per 1,000 (Table 6.3)			
______	×	______	=	$______	(9)

Two Years' Equity with New Loan:

Loan amount		Equity per 1,000			
______	×	______	=	______	(10)

Difference:

Line (10) — Line (9)	$______	(11)

Computing the Bottom Line

To complete the comparison of the two mortgages, you will need to know your marginal rate for federal income taxes. If you are married and file jointly, you can find this rate in the two left columns of Table 6.4. If you are single, look in the two right columns of the same table. If your filing status is different, check with the IRS or your tax adviser.

TABLE 6.4 MARGINAL TAX RATES

Married Couples Filing Joint Returns		Single Persons	
Taxable Income	*Tax Rate*	*Taxable Income*	*Tax Rate*
$17,270–$21,799	.18	$13,920–$16,189	.20
21,800–26,549	.22	16,190–19,639	.23
26,550–32,269	.25	19,640–25,359	.26
32,270–37,979	.28	25,360–31,079	.30
37,980–49,419	.33	31,080–36,799	.34
49,420–64,749	.38	36,800–44,779	.38
64,750–92,369	.42	44,780–59,669	.42
92,370–118,049	.45	59,670–88,269	.48
118,050–175,249	.49	88,270+	.50
175,250+	.50		

Source: Internal Revenue Service.

	Column A	Column B	
Nondeductible Fees: Enter the amount from line (1) on line (12), Column B.		$______	(12)

Net Deductible Fees: The points and interest in arrears you pay can reduce your federal income taxes. The cost to you—the amount paid over and above your tax deduction—is called *net deductible fees.*

To calculate the net cost of points, first figure how much is deductible in the first two years of the mortgage. Enter the amount of the point fee from line (2a). Multiply this by 2 (for the first two years of the loan) and divide it by the number of years on the mortage.

Line (2a):
Years of mortage: × 2 ÷ _____
Deductible points: $_______ (13a)

To calculate the tax deduction, multiply by your tax rate from Table 6.4

Line (13a): __________
Tax rate: × _________
Tax deduction: __________

Column A **Column B**

To figure net deductible points, subtract the tax deduction from the total points on line (2a). Enter your answer on line (13), Column B.

Line (2):

Tax deduction: =________ $________ (13b)

FHA borrowers should calculate the net cost of interest in arrears. If you paid no interest in arrears, enter 0 on line (13c). First, figure the tax deduction. Enter the amount from line (2b). Multiply this by your tax rate.

Line (2b):

Tax rate: ×________

Tax deduction:

To figure net deductible interest in arrears, subtract the tax deduction from the total interest in arrears on line (2b). Enter your answer on line (13c), Column B.

Line (2a):

Tax deduction: =________ $________ (13c)

	Column A	Column B	

Lost Interest: When money is taken out of the bank to pay loan fees, interest is lost. To figure the amount of lost interest, add line (12) and lines (13b) and (13c) to find the total cost of loan fees. Multiply this total by 0.1729 (the compounded rate you would earn on a two-year investment at 8 percent—a reasonable yield on a two-year certificate of deposit). Enter your answer on line (14), Column B.

Line (12):

Lines (13b) + (13c): + ____________

Total cost:

Total cost:

× 0.1729 ______ $________ (14)

Lost Tax Benefits: Because you will be paying less mortgage interest with a lower-rate loan, you will lose some tax benefits. To figure the amount of this loss, multiply the amount from line (5) by your tax rate (from Table 6.4). Enter this amount on line (15), Column B.

Line (5):

Tax rate: × __________ $________ (15)

	Column A	Column B	
Change in Monthly Payments: To figure the total change in monthly payments over two years, multiply the amount in line (8) by 24. If this amount is positive, enter it in Column A of line (16). If it is negative, enter it as a *positive* number in Column B of line (16).			
Line (8): × 24	$______	$______	(16)
Interest Gained on Savings: This assumes that you put the cash difference between the old, high-cost monthly payment and the refinanced loan payment in the bank, where it earned eight percent interest. To figure interest gained on savings, multiply the amount from line (16) by 0.091 (the rate you would earn over two years by investing the difference each month at eight percent). If your answer on line (16) was entered in Column A, enter this answer in Column A of line (17). If your answer on line (16) was entered in Column B, enter this answer in Column B of line (17).			
Line (16): × 0.091	$______	$______	(17)

	Column A	Column B	
Gain of Equity: If you went to a 15-year mortgage from a 30-year mortgage, you could be building equity much faster. Even within the same length of mortgage, equity builds up faster with lower-rate loans. In Column A of line (18), enter the amount from line (11).	$________		(18)
Total Benefits and Costs: Add all the amounts in Column A and enter the total on line (19). These are the financial *benefits* of the refinancing arrangement.	$________		(19)
Add all the amounts in Column B and enter the total on line (20). These are the financial *costs* of the refinancing arrangement.		$________	(20)
The Bottom Line: To determine what the net result would be two years after refinancing, subtract the Column B total from the Column A total. Enter the difference on line (21):			
Line (19) — Line (20)		$________	(21)

This shows the net cash savings—or loss, if the number is negative—two years after refinancing with the new loan you have considered.

7

Ray and Rhonda Ranch

Ray and Rhonda Ranch shaved two percentage points off their FHA-insured mortgage when they refinanced the loan on their raised ranch home in suburbia.

"We're happy," said Rhonda. "We'll recoup our refinancing costs in slightly more than two years, and we'll save nearly $100 a month after that." And they will be picking up equity at a slightly faster clip.

Although they have a joint income of $53,000, Ray and Rhonda wanted to chop the $640 monthly principal and interest payment on their old $62,200 mortgage at 12 percent. With real estate taxes and insurance, the couple was paying nearly $800 a month for housing, not including utilities. So, they traded in their old loan for a 30-year FHA mortgage at 10 percent and now are paying $546 for principal and interest.

"It's frustrating to live in a house with a nearly $800 mortgage payment and know your neighbors, who've been there 20 years or more, are living in an identical home for probably $200 a month," said Rhonda. Not only were interest rates comfortably in single digits when the old-timers bought, but home prices were much lower.

Refinancing can offset only part of the difference, the Ranches know. But assuming continued increases in home prices, in 10 or 15 years new homeowners may look jealously at the Ranches' monthly payments.

"We refinanced because we felt rates wouldn't drop much lower," Rhonda said. First the couple checked with their current lender, but the Ranches' bank didn't offer a particularly good deal. "I figured it's their loss, since we took our business elsewhere," Rhonda said.

The Ranches' timing was excellent. They shopped around and locked in a commitment at 10 percent for 60 days. Because market pressures were pushing rates lower, one lender was charging zero points the day they applied. Points on FHA loans at competitive rates usually run 2 percent to 4 percent of the loan amount.

"It was a hassle to keep phoning different institutions for information—some were reluctant to answer all our questions over the phone," said Rhonda, who made most of the telephone inquiries. "Plus, rates kept changing, so we had to call some places back more than once to be sure we felt we were getting the best deal."

However, once they settled on a lender, their refinancing problems were minimal, they said. "People should not be afraid to ask as many questions as possible and find out as much as they can before they pick a mortgage company or bank," Rhonda said.

RAY AND RHONDA RANCH'S COSTS OF REFINANCING

The worksheet shows how much Ray and Rhonda spent to refinance, and what they saved.

WORKSHEET

FIGURING THE COSTS

Nondeductible Costs

Title Search	$ 490	
Title Insurance	______	
Credit Report	______	
Lawyer Fee	______	
Reappraisal Fee	______	
Loan Origination Fee	622	
Prepayment Penalty	______	
Application Fee	______	
Recording Taxes	180	
Mortgage Insurance	______	
Other Fees: Survey/Inspection	95	
Total Nondeductible Fees	$ 1,387	(1)

Tax-Deductible Costs

Total Point Fee:

Loan amount (thousands) ______ × Points charged 0 × 10 = $ 0 (2a)

Interest in Arrears $ 613 (2b)

Comparing Costs of Two Loans

Old rate: 12% New rate: 10%

Loan amount (thousands): 62.2 Estimated annual income: $53,000

Interest Paid for First Two Years

Two Years' Interest on Old Loan:

Loan amount (thousands)		Interest (from Table 6.1)			
62.2	×	239	=	$14,865.80	(3)

Two Years' Interest on New Loan:

Loan amount		Interest			
62.2	×	199	=	12,377.80	(4)

Difference:

Line (3) — Line (4) $2,488.00 (5)

Monthly Payments

Monthly Payment for Old Loan:

Loan amount (thousands)		Cost per 1,000 (Table 6.2)			
62.2	×	10.29	=	$640.04	(6)

Monthly Payment for New Loan:

Loan amount		Cost per 1,000			
62.2	×	8.78	=	540.12	(7)

Difference:

Line (6) — Line (7) $99.92 (8)

Equity Buildup After Two Years

Two Years' Equity with Old Loan:

Loan amount (thousands)		Equity per 1,000 (Table 6.3)			
62.2	×	8	=	$497.60	(9)

Two Years' Equity with New Loan:

Loan amount		Equity per 1,000			
62.2	×	12	=	746.40	(10)

Difference:

Line (10) — Line (9) $248.80 (11)

COMPUTING THE BOTTOM LINE

	Column A	Column B	
Nondeductible Fees			
From line (1)		$ 1,387	(12)
Net Deductible Fees			
Part of points deductible:			
Line (2a): 0			
Years of mortgage: × 2 ÷ ____			
Deductible points:		$____	(13a)
Tax Deduction on Points			
Line (13a):			
Tax rate: × ____			
Tax deduction:			
Net Deductible Points			
Line (2a):			
Tax deduction: − ____		$ 0	(13b)
Interest in Arrears:			
Tax deduction:			
Line (2b): 613			
Tax rate: × .38			
Tax deduction: 232.94			
Net Deductible Interest in Arrears:			
Line (2a): 613			
Tax deduction: 232.94		380.06	(13c)

	Column A	Column B	
Lost Interest			
Line (12): 1,387			
Lines (13b) + (13c): 380.06			
Total cost: 1,767.06			
Total cost: × 0.1729		$ 305.52	(14)
Lost Tax Benefits			
Line (5): 2,488			
Tax rate: × .38		$ 945.44	(15)
Change in Monthly Payments			
Line (8): 93.92 × 24	$ 2,254.08	$ ______	(16)
(Positive answer in Column A; negative answer in Column B.)			
Interest Gained on Savings			
Line (16): 2,254.08 × 0.091	$ 205.12	$ ______	(17)
(In same column as answer on line (16).)			
Gain of Equity			
From line (11)	$ 248.80		(18)

	Column A	Column B	
Total Benefits and Costs			
Total of Column A	$2,708.00		(19)
Total of Column B		$3,018.02	(20)
The Bottom Line			
Line (19) — Line (20)		$-310.02	(21)

CONCLUSIONS

Perhaps the most unusual aspect of the Ranches' refinancing is that they did not have to pay points. When an FHA loan is refinanced, another quirk is interest in arrears, which must be paid at closing. It cost the couple $613, which the Ranches can deduct when filing their federal income taxes.

Also, they had to pay a loan origination fee of 1 percent of the loan amount, or $622. This fee is not tax deductible. However, when the Ranches sell the house they will be able to subtract all nondeductible closing fees from the profit they make on the dwelling.

Within two years the Ranches will be able to offset all but $310.02 of their closing costs and lost interest deductions because of the $93.92 monthly payment savings. Several months into the third year of the new loan, they will be ahead. If the Ranches stay in their home 10 years, their refinancing investment will have paid a dividend of thousands of dollars—and their neighbors will look jealously at their $546.12 monthly principal and interest payment.

8
Bob and Barbara Bungalow

Bob and Barbara Bungalow bought a vintage three-bedroom brick home in an up-and-coming city neighborhood. They took out a $70,000 mortgage at 13 percent for 15 years. They have a combined taxable income of $55,000.

As rates began to drop, the couple thought it would be worth the hassle to refinance and cut their monthly mortgage payments.

Another motivation was the possibility of getting rid of the burden of a monthly fee of about $35 for private mortgage insurance (PMI). When they took out their original loan they were able to come up with only a 17 percent down payment, instead of the 20 percent necessary to avoid PMI.

Barbara knew more about the financing game than Bob, because she and a friend had been investors in a two-flat (duplex or double-bungalow) before she was married.

"The previous mortgage I had on the two-flat was 15.75 percent. Bob was a first-time buyer. He was shocked at points and other costs of financing a home," Barbara said. They chose to refinance with another $70,000 mortgage for 15 years, but because rates had fallen to 10.5 percent, the monthly principal and interest payment dropped to $773 from $885—a savings of $112 a month.

The Bungalows avoided PMI on the refinancing because a reappraisal showed the value of their house had appreciated enough to bring their equity up to 20 percent. This saved another $35 a month, so the Bungalows actually pocketed savings of $147 a month. To make comparison easier, the worksheet that follows shows only the $112 difference.

Besides the lower payments, a lower interest rate means that equity on their home also will build up faster.

"We refinanced so we wouldn't be wasting money," said Barbara. "Our goal was to pay off our credit card debts at 18 percent and higher with money we saved on monthly payments."

The Bungalows said their timing was right. "Procrastination paid off for us," Barbara said. "We waited for four months before refinancing, and rates dropped lower. We were hoping rates would fall to 10 percent (later they did) but figured it wasn't worth the risk of waiting for another half a percentage point. My mother, a Florida real estate broker, advised us to wait. She thought rates would go lower, and they did. But if we would have waited too long and missed the lower rates, we might have ended up stuck with the 13 percent loan."

The refinancing hassle was minimized because the Bungalows decided to go back to the lender who made their earlier loan. The refinancing cut 2.5 points off the Bungalows' interest rate, but they had to pay 2.5 percent of the loan amount, or $1,750, in points.

To help defray costs, the couple timed their refinancing to coincide with a $1,900 federal income-tax refund. "If we didn't get the tax refund in time, we were prepared to borrow money for points and closing costs," Barbara said.

If the IRS hadn't come through, Bob said another potential source of money for closing costs was a short-term cash advance from MasterCard which the Bungalows would have paid off immediately after the refund arrived. But this was a last resort because of the high interest rate charged for plastic credit.

"We're happy we refinanced. Now we have more spendable income to clear up our debts," Barbara said. "We both were swimming in debt because of Christmas gifts bought on credit."

BOB AND BARBARA BUNGALOW'S COSTS OF REFINANCING

The worksheet shows how much Bob and Barbara spent to refinance and what they saved.

WORKSHEET

FIGURING THE COSTS

Nondeductible Costs

Title Search	$ 15	
Title Insurance	400	
Credit Report	______	
Lawyer Fee	150	
Reappraisal Fee	______	
Loan Origination Fee	______	
Prepayment Penalty	______	
Application Fee	250	
Recording Taxes	64	
Mortgage Insurance	______	
Other Fees: ________	______	
Total Nondeductible Fees	$ 879	(1)

Tax-Deductible Costs

Total Point Fee:

Loan amount (thousands)		Points charged				
70	×	2.5	× 10	=	$ 1,750	(2a)
Interest in Arrears					$ 0	(2b)

Comparing Costs of Two Loans

Old rate: 13% New rate: 10.5%

Loan amount (thousands): 70 Estimated annual income: $55,000

Two Years' Interest on Old Loan:

Loan amount (thousands)		Interest (from Table 6.1)			
70	×	254	=	$17,780	(3)

Two Years' Interest on New Loan:

Loan amount		Interest			
70	×	204	=	14,280	(4)

Difference:

Line (3) — Line (4) $3,500 (5)

Monthly Payments

Monthly Payment for Old Loan:

Loan amount (thousands)		Cost per 1,000 (Table 6.2)			
70	×	12.66	=	$886.20	(6)

Monthly Payment for New Loan:

Loan amount		Cost per 1,000			
70	×	11.06	=	774.20	(7)

Difference:

Line (6) — Line (7) $112.00 (8)

Equity Buildup After Two Years

Two Years' Equity with Old Loan:

Loan amount (thousands)		Equity per 1,000 (Table 6.3)			
70	×	50	=	$3,500	(9)

Two Years' Equity with New Loan:

Loan amount		Equity per 1,000			
70	×	61	=	4,270	(10)

Difference:

Line (10) — Line (9) $770 (11)

COMPUTING THE BOTTOM LINE

	Column A	Column B	
Nondeductible Fees			
From line (1)		$ 879	(12)
Net Deductible Fees			
Part of points deductible:			
Line (2a): 1,750			
Years of mortgage: × 2 ÷ 15			
Deductible points:		$ 233.33	(13a)
Tax Deduction on Points			
Line (13a): 233.33			
Tax rate: × .38			
Tax deduction: 88.67			
Net Deductible Points			
Line (2a): 1,750			
Tax deduction: − 88.67		$ 1,661.33	(13b)
Interest in Arrears:			
Tax deduction:			
Line (2b): ______			
Tax rate: × ______			
Tax deduction: ______			
Net Deductible Interest in Arrears:			
Line (2a): ______			
Tax deduction: ______		0	(13c)

	Column A	Column B	
Lost Interest			
Line (12): 879.00 Lines (13b) + (13c): 1,661.33 Total cost: 2,540.33			
Total cost: 2,540.33 × 0.1729		$ 439.22	(14)
Lost Tax Benefits			
Line (5): 3,500 Tax rate: × .38		$ 1,330	(15)
Change in Monthly Payments			
Line (8): 112 × 24	$ 2,688	$ ______	(16)
(Positive answer in Column A; negative answer in Column B.)			
Interest Gained on Savings			
Line (16): 2,688 × 0.091	$ 244.61	$ ______	(17)
(In same column as answer on line (16).)			
Gain of Equity			
From line (11)	$ 770		(18)

	Column A	Column B	
Total Benefits and Costs			
Total of Column A	$3,702.61		(19)
Total of Column B		$4,309.55	(20)
The Bottom Line			
Line (19) — Line (20)		$-606.94	(21)

CONCLUSIONS

The May, 1986, IRS decision to spread the deduction of points over the life of the loan means that the Bungalows won't be able to break even until the third year of their refinanced mortgage.

Through refinancing, the couple will save $2,688 in lower monthly payments, earn $244 on that savings, and add $770 in equity buildup over the first two years of the loan. That's a total of $3,702.

Bob and Barbara's added equity means they own more of their home. More good news is that the difference won't show up in their checking account until they sell the home or borrow against their equity.

The Bungalows' refinancing costs were $2,540.33 in after-tax points and closing fees, $439 in foregone interest, and $1,330 in lost income-tax deductions. That's a total of $4,309.55.

All told, the Bungalows would be $606.94 in the hole after two years. But figuring in a $35 monthly savings by ridding themselves of the burden of PMI payments—$840 over two years— the Bungalows will actually be $233.06 ahead after two years.

Refinancing will pay off quickly for the Bungalows. After two years, the costs already will be covered and the gains will begin to mount.

9
Bill and Betty Balloon

Bill and Betty Balloon bought a four-bedroom multilevel home on a wooded acre in a posh suburb. With taxable income of $60,000, they had no trouble qualifying with a local savings and loan association for a $97,000, five-year balloon loan at 12.25 percent.

But Bill and Betty never felt comfortable with the balloon loan. They were aware that although it was amortized over 30 years, in five years they would have to pay the entire balance due. This requirement meant that when the loan came due, the Balloons would have to renegotiate or take the prevailing rate on a new mortgage.

When rates dropped, 18 months into the loan, Bill and Betty shopped around and found a mortgage company offering a 30-year fixed-rate loan at 10.25 percent. Closing fees were three points. Under the 30-year plan, the Balloons will save $148.41 a month in principal and interest payments.

The home had appreciated in value, so they had considered taking out a new mortgage of $102,000. The extra cash would go to financing the three-point service charge—roughly $3,000—and the other costs involved: attorney, title insurance, survey, well and septic inspection, appraisal and credit check, and a mortgage processing charge. Plus, they would have more than $1,000 to pay off credit-card debt.

But they didn't want to pay back three times what they borrowed, so they kept the mortgage amount the same.

Because the rates had dropped, the Balloons also considered switching to a 15-year mortgage from their current loan. They decided against it because they didn't want to tie up so much of their money each month. If they choose to, they can prepay principal on their 30-year loan, but they aren't locked into the larger payments of a 15-year loan.

"We wanted a mortgage with a longer term than a five-year balloon. And, as everyone does, we wanted to lower our monthly payments," said Bill. "The day after we committed to the 10.25 percent loan, rates bounced back up to 11 percent, but later they went lower. Now, however, I wish we would have waited for something in the 9-percent range. I never dreamed rates would get down even lower. But you can't be greedy."

Bill and Betty's involvement in the refinancing process kept hassles to a minimum. "The mortagage broker was eager to please," said Bill. "He came to our house to fill out the application, and generally made sure things went smoothly. But I really believe that we avoided problems by handling a lot of it ourselves."

A licensed real estate salesperson, Bill ordered his own well and septic inspection, negotiated an update charge from a surveyor, shopped around for the least costly title insurance, ordered his own mortgage payout letter, and supplied the appraiser with resale values of comparable homes.

"I made sure the lender had everything he needed, so there weren't any last-minute hangups," Bill said.

Twenty-eight days later, the mortgage was approved and a closing date was arranged.

Bill gave the following refinancing advice to novice homeowners: "People should closely examine the numbers on the various documents they are confronted with at closing. I did, and found that what I was being charged for title insurance was about $150 too much."

Refinancing was so easy, Bill said, he and Betty may do it again if the rates continue to plunge.

BILL AND BETTY BALLOON'S COSTS OF REFINANCING

The worksheet shows how much Bill and Betty spent to refinance, and what they saved.

WORKSHEET

FIGURING THE COSTS

Nondeductible Costs

Title Search	$ 435	
Title Insurance	____	
Credit Report	50	
Lawyer Fee	200	
Reappraisal Fee	200	
Loan Origination Fee	____	
Prepayment Penalty	____	
Application Fee	____	
Recording Taxes	25	
Mortgage Insurance	____	
Other Fees: Mortgage processing	255	
Total Nondeductible Fees	$ 1,165	(1)

Tax-Deductible Costs

Total Point Fee:

Loan amount (thousands)		Points charged					
97	×	3	× 10	=	$ 2,910	(2a)

Interest in Arrears $ 0 (2b)

Comparing Costs of Two Loans

Old rate: 12.5% New rate: 10.5%

Loan amount (thousands): 97 Estimated annual income: $60,000

Interest Paid for First Two Years

Two Years' Interest on Old Loan:

Loan amount (thousands)		Interest (from Table 6.1)			
97	×	249	=	$24,153	(3)

Two Years' Interest on New Loan:

Loan amount		Interest			
97	×	209	=	20,273	(4)

Difference:

Line (3) — Line (4) $3,880 (5)

Monthly Payments

Monthly Payment for Old Loan:

Loan amount (thousands)		Cost per 1,000 (Table 6.2)			
97	×	10.68	=	$1,035.96	(6)

Monthly Payment for New Loan:

Loan amount		Cost per 1,000			
97	×	9.15	=	887.55	(7)

Difference:

Line (6) — Line (7) $148.41 (8)

Equity Buildup After Two Years

Two Years' Equity with Old Loan:

Loan amount (thousands)		Equity per 1,000 (Table 6.3)			
97	×	7	=	$679	(9)

Two Years' Equity with New Loan:

Loan amount		Equity per 1,000			
97	×	11	=	1,067	(10)

Difference:

Line (10) — Line (9) $388 (11)

COMPUTING THE BOTTOM LINE

	Column A	Column B	
Nondeductible Fees			
From line (1)		$ 1,165	(12)
Net Deductible Fees			
Part of points deductible:			
Line (2a): 2,910			
Years of mortgage: × 2 ÷ 30			
Deductible points: 194		$ 194	(13a)
Tax Deduction on Points			
Line (13a): 194			
Tax rate: × .38			
Tax deduction: 73.72			
Net Deductible Points			
Line (2a): 2,910			
Tax deduction: − 73.72		$ 2,836.28	(13b)
Interest in Arrears:			
Tax deduction:			
Line (2b): 0			
Tax rate: × ______			
Tax deduction: ______			
Net Deductible Interest in Arrears:			
Line (2a): ______			
Tax deduction: ______		0	(13c)

	Column A	Column B	
Lost Interest			
Line (12): 1,165			
Lines (13b) + (13c): 2,836.28			
Total cost: 4,001.28			
Total cost: 4,001.28 × 0.1729		$691.82	(14)
Lost Tax Benefits			
Line (5): 3,880			
Tax rate: × .38		$1,474.40	(15)
Change in Monthly Payments			
Line (8): 148.41 × 24	$3,561.84	$______	(16)
(Positive answer in Column A; negative answer in Column B.)			
Interest Gained on Savings			
Line (16): 3,561.84 × 0.091	$324.13	$______	(17)
(In same column as answer on line (16).)			
Gain of Equity			
From line (11)	$388		(18)

	Column A	Column B	
Total Benefits and Costs			
Total of Column A	$4,273.97		(19)
Total of Column B		$6,167.50	(20)
The Bottom Line			
Line (19) — Line (20)		$-1,893.53	(21)

CONCLUSIONS

The sharp decline in interest rates was a godsend for the Balloons. Uncomfortable with the prospect of having to accept a high-rate mortgage when their balloon popped, the couple were eager to refinance. Like other families with balloons, they wisely locked in an affordable rate when the opportunity arose.

The costs of refinancing for the Balloons may seem high to other homeowners, but most fees are tied to the size of the loan. Also, the Balloons had to pay three points, which is slightly above average. On the $97,000 loan, the points cost $2,910.

Another major negative of the Balloons' refinancing arrangement is the $1,474.40 loss of tax benefits caused by the lower interest rate. Again, the size of the mortgage amplified this.

The major savings of refinancing was the $148.41 reduction in the monthly payment. Also, the lower rate allowed an increase in equity of $388.

After two years, the Balloons will be $683 from breaking even. And about four months into year three, they will be on their way to a profitable arrangement—and much more comfortable with a long-term mortgage than with a balloon.

10
Carl Condo

Carl Condo, a divorcé who earns $49,500 a year, had a 30-year, $34,500 mortgage at 13 percent on his one-bedroom condominium in the city. He traded this mortgage for a 15-year fixed-rate loan at 9.5 percent.

When he refinanced for $34,000, his monthly payment dropped only $26 to $355 from $381, but Carl substantially increased the rate of future equity buildup. His refinancing costs totaled $1,445 for points and closing fees.

Carl lost tax savings of $1,125 when the mortgage interest deduction declined by $2,680 over two years. But he said the trade-off was worth it because he hopes to move and rent the condo. The slightly lower monthly principal and interest cost will make it easier for him to break even or earn a positive cash flow from the unit.

"I refinanced because the reduction in interest rates was too good to pass up," said Carl. "I decided to make a move if I could knock three percentage points off my rate. It turned out better than I imagined."

Carl's refinancing went very smoothly; it was much easier than getting the original loan. "It was well worth it," he said.

"When I took out my mortgage, I thought rates were headed up even higher. I thought I was doing well at the time. Now, I actually can imagine the day when I will own the unit outright."

Although the timing of his refinancing was nearly perfect, Carl, a middle-aged executive, admitted he "didn't know what I was doing. The bank loan officer helped a lot. She explained everything and made it easy for me."

At the lender's suggestion, Carl decided to take responsibility for his own real estate taxes instead of letting the bank put the money into escrow. "I'll earn interest on the money, but I'll leave it in her bank as a courtesy," Carl said.

CARL CONDO'S COSTS OF REFINANCING

The worksheet shows how much Carl spent to refinance, and what he saved.

WORKSHEET

FIGURING THE COSTS

Nondeductible Costs

Title Search	$ 60	
Title Insurance	150	
Credit Report		
Lawyer Fee	225	
Reappraisal Fee		
Loan Origination Fee		
Prepayment Penalty		
Application Fee		
Recording Taxes	30	
Mortgage Insurance		
Other Fees: Settlement fee	80	
Total Nondeductible Fees	$ 595	(1)

Tax-Deductible Costs

Total Point Fee:

Loan amount (thousands)		Points charged					
34	×	2.5	× 10	=	$ 850	(2a)

Interest in Arrears $ 0 (2b)

Comparing Costs of Two Loans

Old rate: 13% New rate: 9.5%

Loan amount (thousands): 34 Estimated annual income: $49,500

Interest Paid for First Two Years

Two Years' Interest on Old Loan:

Loan amount (thousands)		Interest (from Table 6.1)			
34.5	×	260	=	$8,970	(3)

Two Years' Interest on New Loan:

Loan amount		Interest			
34	×	185	=	6,290	(4)

Difference:

Line (3) — Line (4) $2,680 (5)

Monthly Payments

Monthly Payment for Old Loan:

Loan amount (thousands)		Cost per 1,000 (Table 6.2)			
34.5	×	11.07	=	$381.92	(6)

Monthly Payment for New Loan:

Loan amount		Cost per 1,000			
34	×	10.45	=	355.30	(7)

Difference:

Line (6) — Line (7) $26.62 (8)

Equity Buildup After Two Years

Two Years' Equity with Old Loan:

Loan amount (thousands)		Equity per 1,000 (Table 6.3)			
34.5	×	6	=	$207	(9)

Two Years' Equity with New Loan:

Loan amount		Equity per 1,000			
34	×	66	=	2,244	(10)

Difference:

Line (10) — Line (9) $2,037 (11)

COMPUTING THE BOTTOM LINE

	Column A	Column B
Nondeductible Fees		
From line (1)		$ 595 (12)
Net Deductible Fees		
Part of points deductible:		
Line (2a): 850		
Years of mortgage: × 2 ÷ 15		
Deductible points: 113.33		$ 113.33 (13a)
Tax Deduction on Points		
Line (13a): 113.33		
Tax rate: × .42		
Tax deduction: 47.60		
Net Deductible Points		
Line (2a): 850		
Tax deduction: − 47.60		$ 802.40 (13b)
Interest in Arrears:		
Tax deduction:		
Line (2b): ________		
Tax rate: × ________		
Tax deduction: ________		
Net Deductible Interest in Arrears:		
Line (2a): ________		
Tax deduction: ________		0 (13c)

	Column A	Column B	
Lost Interest			
Line (12): 595			
Lines (13b) + (13c): 802.40			
Total cost: 1,397.40			
Total cost: 1,397.40 × 0.1729		$241.61	(14)
Lost Tax Benefits			
Line (5): 2,680 Tax rate: × .42		$1,125.60	(15)
Change in Monthly Payments			
Line (8): 26.62 × 24	$638.88	$	(16)
(Positive answer in Column A; negative answer in Column B.)			
Interest Gained on Savings			
Line (16): 638.88 × 0.091	$58.14	$	(17)
(In same column as answer on line (16).)			
Gain of Equity			
From line (11)	$2,037		(18)

	Column A	Column B	
Total Benefits and Costs			
Total of Column A	$2,734.02		(19)
Total of Column B		$2,764.61	(20)
The Bottom Line			
Line (19) — Line (20)		$-30.59	(21)

CONCLUSIONS

At first glance, Carl Condo's refinancing arrangement doesn't look like such a good idea. His monthly payment, after all, decreased only $26 to $355—and he ended up paying after-tax costs of $1,397.40 to do it. But look a little closer.

Even this small monthly saving builds fast—into $638 in two years. Also, the switch to a 15-year mortgage means Carl's equity in his condo will increase 10 times faster than under his old 30-year loan. *Instead of $207, Carl will have $2,037.*

Clearly, this arrangement will pay off quickly for Carl. In fact, he will be within $30.59 of breaking even after two years. Then, the savings wil start to pile up.

11
Tony and Theresa Twoflat

A couple of years ago, Tony and Theresa Twoflat took out a 30-year fixed-rate mortgage at 13 percent. At the time, they figured they were in for the long term. Interest rates seemed stable then.

But when rates dropped sharply in late 1985 and 1986, the couple traded the $70,000 mortgage on their two-flat apartment building in the city for a 15-year fixed-rate loan at 10 percent. Because they were taking a shorter-term mortgage, their $774 monthly principal and interest payment dropped only to $752.

Because the reappraisal showed their property had appreciated since they bought it, the couple's equity in the building increased to 20 percent of the two-flat's value. As a result, on the new loan they were not required to pay private mortgage insurance. This saved them another $16 a month.

The Twoflats paid $2,378 in points and closing fees, but the equity buildup gained from the switch to a 15-year loan was well worth the expense. The couple picked up a whopping $4,060 more in equity in just two years than they would have gotten on their old 30-year loan.

"Lower rates prompted us to refinance," said Theresa. "It definitely was worth it. Our timing was right. Rates had fallen far enough to make it worthwhile, and we didn't think they'd go lower soon."

Tony said refinancing was very easy. "The mortgage broker even came to our house to take the application."

The Twoflats said the lender had to hustle to get all their paperwork done in time for the closing because of the backlog caused by so many people refinancing.

They shopped around and refinanced with a reliable mortgage broker. Rates were competitive and points generally were lower there. "I saved one point ($700) over similar rates offered by banks and savings and loans."

The Twoflats also helped themselves by asking questions. "I saved money on the survey by asking the lender to deal with the firm that did the initial survey," Tony said.

However, there also were problems caused by the heavy inflow of refinancing applications. "My title search accidentally was billed at nearly twice the normal cost," he said.

Tony urged families who plan to refinance to consider having the appraisal on their property boosted to eliminate the extra cost of PMI payments, which can build up surprisingly fast. "The real estate agent who sold you the house may be able to help find higher comparable values of properties similar to yours," he said.

TONY AND THERESA TWOFLAT'S COSTS OF REFINANCING

The worksheet shows how much Tony and Theresa spent to refinance, and what they saved.

WORKSHEET

FIGURING THE COSTS

Nondeductible Costs

Title Search	$ 355.50
Title Insurance	______
Credit Report	42.90
Lawyer Fee	______
Reappraisal Fee	300
Loan Origination Fee	______
Prepayment Penalty	______
Application Fee	______
Recording Taxes	36
Mortgage Insurance	______
Other Fees: ________	244
Total Nondeductible Fees	$ 978.40 (1)

Tax-Deductible Costs

Total Point Fee:

Loan amount (thousands)		Points charged				
70	×	2	× 10	=	$ 1,400	(2a)

Interest in Arrears $ 0 (2b)

Comparing Costs of Two Loans

Old rate: 13% New rate: 10%

Loan amount (thousands): 70 Estimated annual income: $38,000

Interest Paid for First Two Years

Two Years' Interest on Old Loan:

Loan amount (thousands)		Interest (from Table 6.1)			
70	×	260	=	$18,200	(3)

Two Years' Interest on New Loan:

Loan amount		Interest			
70	×	174	=	13,580	(4)

Difference:

Line (3) — Line (4) $4,620 (5)

Monthly Payments

Monthly Payment for Old Loan:

Loan amount (thousands)		Cost per 1,000 (Table 6.2)			
70	×	11.07	=	$774.90	(6)

Monthly Payment for New Loan:

Loan amount		Cost per 1,000			
70	×	10.75	=	752.50	(7)

Difference:

Line (6) — Line (7) $22.40 (8)

Equity Buildup After Two Years

Two Years' Equity with Old Loan:

Loan amount (thousands)		Equity per 1,000 (Table 6.3)			
70	×	6	=	$420	(9)

Two Years' Equity with New Loan:

Loan amount		Equity per 1,000			
70	×	64	=	4,480	(10)

Difference:

Line (10) — Line (9) $4,060 (11)

COMPUTING THE BOTTOM LINE

	Column A	Column B

Nondeductible Fees

From line (1) $ 978.40 (12)

Net Deductible Fees

Part of points deductible:

Line (2a): 1,400

Years of mortgage: × 2 ÷ 15

Deductible points: 186.67 $ 186.67 (13a)

Tax Deduction on Points

Line (13a): 186.67

Tax rate: × .33

Tax deduction: 61.60

Net Deductible Points

Line (2a): 1,400

Tax deduction: − 61.60 $ 1,388.40 (13b)

Interest in Arrears:

Tax deduction: 0

Line (2b): ________

Tax rate: × ________

Tax deduction: ________

Net Deductible Interest in Arrears:

Line (2a): ________

Tax deduction: ________ 0 (13c)

	Column A	Column B	
Lost Interest			
Line (12): 978.40			
Lines (13b) + (13c): 1,338.40			
Total cost: 2,316.80			
Total cost: 2,316.80 × 0.1729		$ 400.57	(14)
Lost Tax Benefits			
Line (5): 4,620			
Tax rate: × .33		$ 1,524.60	(15)
Change in Monthly Payments			
Line (8): 22.40 × 24	$ 537.60	$	(16)
(Positive answer in Column A; negative answer in Column B.)			
Interest Gained on Savings			
Line (16): 537.60 × 0.091	$ 48.92	$	(17)
(In same column as answer on line (16).)			
Gain of Equity			
From line (11)	$ 4,060		(18)

	Column A	Column B	
Total Benefits and Costs			
Total of Column A	$4,646.52		(19)
Total of Column B		$4,241.97	(20)
The Bottom Line			
Line (19) — Line (20)		$ 404.55	(21)

CONCLUSIONS

If ever there was a couple that should refinance, it's Tony and Theresa Twoflat. Not only are their monthly payments lower than with the old 30-year loan, but they will build an astounding $4,060 in additional equity after making payments for only two years on their 15-year mortgage.

By shopping around, they were able to find a mortgage that required only two points. The savings on points and survey costs mean that the Twoflats can begin profiting from the refinancing within two years of closing.

Added to this rosy picture is the elimination of private mortgage insurance. The Twoflats' refinancing arrangement will produce a $404.55 profit after two years. But that really translates into a profit of $823.55 when PMI is removed.

If lenders ever need an advertisement for the benefits of refinancing, they should ring the Twoflats' door-bell.

CONCLUSION

12
Twenty Common Questions —and Answers— About Refinancing

1. ***What makes refinancing worth the bureaucratic hassles?***

There are two major benefits of refinancing. First, your monthly mortgage payments will go down, often substantially. That leaves more money in your monthly budget for groceries, clothing, home improvements, vacations, or further investments.

Second, you build up equity in a home faster with a lower mortgage rate. That means if you sell the home before the mortgage is paid off, you end up with more money to spend on your next home or to invest.

2. ***Should I refinance now or wait for rates to go lower?***

If you know for sure where rates are going, you should be a millionaire in the bond markets of Wall Street. In mid-1985, economists certainly weren't predicting 9.5 percent fixed-rate loans for early 1986.

In other words, ordinary consumers should grab a rate that makes sense. There's no telling when rates will go up or down. If a refinancing works out to be a good deal, take it and be happy. Maybe you won't save every nickel possible, but you will be way ahead of not refinancing at all. By waiting for the "perfect" time, you may miss the boat.

As wiley investors say on Wall Street: It's one thing to be a bull, another to be a bear—but pigs end up being slaughtered.

3. *Should I "lock in" the interest rate that is in effect when I make my loan application? Is there a fee for this?*

Ask exactly *when* the new rate you are applying for will be established. With rates fluctuating daily, a homeowner should determine whether the new contract rate will be the rate available on the day of the application or the rate available on the day of the actual closing.

Some banks may charge up to a full point extra to permit a homeowner to be locked in to a chosen rate before the actual closing.

4. *How much will it cost to refinance?*

That depends on the lender. When you compare loans from different lenders, look at all costs, not just rates and points. When you talk to a potential lender, ask which of the following fees apply to the loans he or she makes:

- Points;
- Title search;
- Title insurance;
- Application fee;
- Credit report;
- Real estate lawyer fees;
- Reappraisal fee;
- Prepayment penalty;
- Loan origination fee;
- Recording taxes;
- Private mortgage insurance;
- Interest in arrears

5. *Should I switch to a fixed-rate loan from an adjustable-rate mortgage now?*

That question has no simple answer. If you intend to stay in the home another year or two, don't bother refinancing. If your rate is tied to an index that follows interest rates, your adjustable rate won't increase much—and may drop—in the next couple of years.

If, however, you intend to stay in the home for four or more years and want the peace of mind of a fixed rate, go ahead and switch. If you don't mind the risk of fluctuating rates and your budget can absorb payment increases, you may want to stick with the ARM and see where rates go.

Without a crystal ball, it's impossible to tell where rates will be three years from now. With a fixed-rate loan, you know what you'll be paying each and every month for a very long time. With an ARM, you know only the maximum and perhaps the minimum rates you'll be paying—and the maximum is much higher than the current fixed rates.

6. *Should I refinance if I plan to move within two years?*

How certain are those plans? If you are sure you'll be selling the house in two years or less, you probably shouldn't refinance unless you can get a mortgage that would be assumable by the person to whom you sell the house.

If, however, you are only thinking about moving in two years, you should at least consider refinancing. Many Americans are still living in the homes they had planned to move from years ago.

7. *Should I refinance with my current lender?*

You certainly should check with your current lender before refinancing somewhere else. The institution or mortgage company probably wants to keep your business—especially if you have been a prompt payer.

For that reason, the lender may waive some of the fees, reduce the points, and speed along the process. The current lender ordered a credit check on you when you originally received financing there.

However, if another lender is offering a better deal in rate, points, or other fees, take it. That lender may have more money to lend or may be trying to build up business with low rates. Take advantage of this.

8. ***Because lenders seem to be so competitive, aren't all their rates about the same?***

No. Like supermarkets and department stores, lending institutions have different costs and desired profit margins. Also, they try to establish different client bases. Consequently, lenders' offerings can differ in rates, points, and fees.

9. ***How many lenders should I call for loan-rate quotes when shopping for a refinanced mortgage?***

An old rule of thumb was three. That was true in the days of homogeneous lenders and mortgages. In the deregulated and highly competitive market that exists now, three probably are too few.

Why not get out your local phone book and phone every lender in there? Sure, this will take some time. But consider that every $10 saved in monthly payments means 180 or 360 months at $10. That's $1,800 or $3,600 over the course of a 15-year loan or a 30-year loan, respectively. So, calling lots of lenders may be a very good investment.

10. ***How long will it take to close on the new mortgage from the time I make the application?***

It's impossible to say how long this will take, but be prepared for a wait. Lenders are very busy because of the low rates. Once you begin the process, however, you usually can lock in a rate with the lender.

There are a number of things you can do to speed up the process. These include paying the loan application fee immediately, alerting your employer that an employment verification is on the way, getting copies of your tax forms for the last two years, and providing the lender with account numbers and addresses for bank and stock accounts and credit cards. Also, you should give the lender names and addresses on all loans you have paid off.

11. ***On my federal income-tax form, may I deduct the points I pay to refinance?***

In May, 1986, the Internal Revenue Service decided that

homeowners can deduct the points they pay to refinance, but the deduction must be spread evenly over the life of the loan.

So, a borrower who pays $1,500 in points on a refinanced $50,000 mortgage only would be allowed to deduct $50 each year for the 30 years of the loan.

12. ***May I add the cost of points into my refinanced mortgage, thus increasing my loan amount?***

The lender will have no problem allowing this if the home is appraised for a higher value than when the loan originally was made or if you are willing to sacrifice some of the equity you already have in the home. But remember, you repay $3.16 over 30 years for every $1 you borrow at 10 percent.

13. ***Won't I be losing thousands of dollars in interest deductions when I refinance? And won't that increase my income-tax bill on April 15?***

While it's true that your tax-deductible interest will decrease because your interest rate is lower, you should remember that you are paying out less each month and gaining more equity. Look at it this way: Why pay out $100 to save $25 or $38 in taxes (in the 25 and 38 percent tax brackets, respectively)?

14. ***Should I refinance with a 15-year mortgage even though I have a 30-year loan?***

You certainly should consider it. The sharp decline in rates may make payments on a new 15-year loan less than those on your current 30-year loan. And it's amazing how much faster equity is built up in a 15-year loan. That equity is helpful if you plan to move up to a larger home.

Repeating an example from Chapter 3 may make the difference clearer. On a $50,000 loan at 10 percent for 15 years, you would owe $40,650 after five years. Had you chosen a 30-year loan at 10 percent, you would owe $48,300 after five years.

The difference is even more dramatic after 15 years. While you would be done paying for that 15-year loan, you'd still owe $40,850 on the 30-year mortgage.

15. ***Am I better off paying more points at closing to get a lower rate on the loan?***

First, you should realize that the long-run difference between the choices is not all that substantial. Otherwise, the lender would be much less willing to offer more than one choice.

By paying more points, however, you are spending more of your money upfront. But if you prefer to have a smaller monthly obligation, go ahead and do it.

16. ***How does refinancing affect my equity in the home?***

If you add the points to the loan amount, it clearly reduces your equity. If, however, you pay the points separately, you will not reduce the equity and will be getting a lower-rate loan that allows faster equity growth.

17. ***I had an attorney involved in the original closing of my home. Do I need one for the refinancing process?***

You are entering a contract that will obligate you to repay perhaps hundreds of thousands of dollars. You should have an attorney involved in such a substantial undertaking.

18. ***My home's value has appreciated substantially since I bought it, and I would like to get at some of that equity to build a room addition. Should I refinance to do so?***

If you have an "old," low-rate mortgage, it is probably better to leave well enough alone. It would be better to tap your home's equity by using a home-improvement loan, which really is a second mortgage. Rates on these types of loans have fallen, too. Options include both fixed and adjustable rates.

19. ***Since I took out my current mortgage, I've accumulated several thousand dollars in debts from an auto loan and credit cards. Will these debts keep me from qualifying for a refinanced loan?***

As described in Chapter 3, financial institutions have protected themselves by tightening their credit requirements and limiting the total debt borrowers may carry and still receive loan approval. The new limits are 28 percent of *gross* income for mortgage payments and 36 percent for total debt (including credit cards and auto loans, for example).

This means that if your gross income is $2,000 per month, the highest monthly mortgage payment you may qualify for is $560 per month. Your total monthly debt payment cannot exceed $720 per month.

20. ***Why do I have to pay so many points and fees just to refinance a loan I took out a year or two ago?***

For a lender, refinancing is a new mortgage, and borrowers have to pay for originating the loan.

As discussed in Chapter 4, mortgage fees are negotiable. Lenders charge what the market will bear. When rates are low and refinancing activity is high, some lenders cash in. So, shop around.

Appendix

1. *Abridged Mortgage Amortization Tables*
2. *Loan Progress Tables*
3. *Additional Worksheets*
4. *Tables for Worksheet Reference*

HOW TO USE LOAN AMORTIZATION TABLES

Every borrower who's interested in refinancing should know how to use a loan amortization table.

Once you know current interest rates, it's easy to figure out what mortgage payment it will take to pay off a loan over 15 or 30 years.

This is how lenders do it. Look across from the interest rate and down from the mortgage amount. Where they intersect is the monthly payment for principal and interest. For example, a 30-year loan at 10 percent for $60,000 would cost you $526.55 per month for principal and interest.

If your mortgage amount is not one of those listed, this is just a little bit harder to do. Look across from the interest rate to the cost per $1,000 of loan. Then multiply that number by the amount of your loan (in thousands). For example, a 30-year loan at 10 percent would cost $8.78 per $1,000. For a $66,000 loan, it would cost $8.78 × 66, or $579.48

MONTHLY PAYMENTS TO AMORTIZE 15-YEAR FIXED-RATE LOANS

	$1,000	*$40,000*	*$50,000*	*$60,000*	*$70,000*	*$100,000*
8.00%	9.56	382.27	477.83	573.40	668.96	955.66
8.25	9.71	388.06	485.08	582.09	679.10	970.15
8.50	9.85	393.90	492.37	590.85	689.32	984.74
8.75	10.00	399.78	499.73	599.67	699.62	999.45
9.00	10.15	405.71	507.14	608.56	709.99	1014.27
9.25	10.30	411.68	514.60	617.52	720.44	1029.20
9.50	10.45	417.69	522.12	626.54	730.96	1044.23
9.75	10.60	423.75	529.69	635.62	741.56	1059.37
10.00	10.75	429.85	537.31	644.77	752.23	1074.61
10.25	10.90	435.99	544.98	653.98	762.97	1089.96
10.50	11.06	442.16	552.70	663.24	773.78	1105.40
10.75	11.21	448.38	560.48	672.57	784.67	1120.95
11.00	11.37	454.64	568.30	681.96	795.62	1136.60
11.25	11.53	460.94	576.18	691.41	806.65	1152.35
11.50	11.69	467.28	584.10	700.92	817.74	1168.19
11.75	11.85	473.66	592.07	710.48	828.90	1184.14
12.00	12.01	480.07	600.09	720.11	840.12	1200.17
12.50	12.33	493.01	616.27	739.52	862.77	1232.53
13.00	12.66	506.10	632.63	759.15	885.67	1265.25
13.50	12.99	519.33	649.16	779.00	908.83	1298.32
14.00	13.32	532.70	665.88	799.05	932.22	1331.75
14.50	13.66	546.21	682.76	819.31	955.86	1365.51
15.00	14.00	559.84	699.80	839.76	979.72	1399.59

MONTHLY PAYMENTS TO AMORTIZE 30-YEAR FIXED-RATE LOANS

	$1,000	*$40,000*	*$50,000*	*$60,000*	*$70,000*	*$100,000*
8.00%	7.34	293.51	366.89	440.26	513.64	733.77
8.25	7.52	300.51	375.64	450.76	525.89	751.27
8.50	7.69	307.57	384.46	461.35	538.24	768.92
8.75	7.87	314.69	393.36	472.03	550.70	786.71
9.00	8.05	321.85	402.32	482.78	563.24	804.63
9.25	8.23	329.08	411.34	493.61	575.88	822.68
9.50	8.41	336.35	420.43	504.52	588.60	840.86
9.75	8.60	343.67	429.58	515.50	601.41	859.16
10.00	8.78	351.03	438.79	526.55	614.31	877.58
10.25	8.97	358.45	448.06	537.67	627.28	896.11
10.50	9.15	365.90	457.37	548.85	640.32	914.74
10.75	9.34	373.40	466.75	560.09	653.44	933.49
11.00	9.53	380.93	476.17	571.40	666.63	952.33
11.25	9.72	388.51	485.64	582.76	679.89	971.27
11.50	9.91	396.12	495.15	594.18	693.21	990.30
11.75	10.10	403.77	504.71	605.65	706.59	1009.41
12.00	10.29	411.45	514.31	617.17	720.03	1028.62
12.50	10.68	426.91	533.63	640.36	747.09	1067.26
13.00	11.07	442.48	553.10	663.72	774.34	1106.20
13.50	11.46	458.17	572.71	687.25	801.79	1145.42
14.00	11.85	473.95	592.44	710.93	829.42	1184.88
14.50	12.25	489.83	612.28	734.74	857.19	1224.56
15.00	12.65	505.78	632.23	758.67	885.12	1264.45

HOW TO USE LOAN PROGRESS TABLES

This table will help you know how much of your loan will be paid off after set amounts of time have elapsed.

First, find the interest rate of your loan in the left column.

Next, in the second column, find the original term—or length—of your loan. Then run your finger across to the year of the loan that you are interested in. The figure represents the amount of principal remaining to be paid off for each $1,000 of your loan. To find the total remaining principal, multiply this number by the amount of your loan (in thousands).

For example, after five years of a 30-year loan at 10 percent, you would still owe $966 of each $1,000 you borrowed. On a $60,000 loan, you would still owe $966 × 60, or $57,960.

After 20 years on that same 10-percent, 30-year loan, you would still owe $664 of each $1,000 originally borrowed. On that $60,000 loan, you would still owe $664 × 60, or $39,840.

LOAN PROGRESS CHART

Showing the dollar balance remaining per $1000 of loan

INT RATE	ORIG TERM	ELAPSED TERM IN YEARS 2	5	8	10	12	15	18	20	22	25
8⅛%	10	859	600	269							
	15	926	789	615	473	307					
	20	957	877	775	692	595	415	186			
	25	973	924	861	810	750	639	499	384	248	
	30	983	952	912	879	841	771	682	609	523	365
8¼%	10	860	601	271							
	15	927	791	617	476	308					
	20	957	878	777	695	597	418	188			
	25	974	925	863	813	753	643	502	387	251	
	30	983	953	914	882	844	774	685	613	527	368
8⅜%	10	861	603	272							
	15	927	793	620	478	310					
	20	958	880	780	697	600	420	189			
	25	974	927	865	815	756	646	505	390	253	
	30	984	954	915	884	847	778	689	616	530	372
8½%	10	861	604	273							
	15	928	794	622	480	312					
	20	958	881	782	700	603	423	191			
	25	975	928	867	818	759	649	508	392	255	
	30	984	955	917	886	849	781	693	620	534	375
8⅝%	10	862	606	274							
	15	929	796	624	482	314					
	20	959	883	784	703	606	426	192			
	25	975	929	869	820	762	653	512	395	257	
	30	985	956	919	888	852	784	696	624	538	378
8¾%	10	863	607	275							
	15	929	797	626	484	315					
	20	960	884	786	705	609	428	194			
	25	976	930	871	823	765	656	515	398	259	
	30	985	957	920	890	854	787	700	628	542	381
8⅞%	10	864	609	276							
	15	930	799	628	486	317					
	20	960	886	788	708	611	431	195			
	25	976	932	873	825	767	659	518	401	262	
	30	985	958	922	892	857	790	703	631	546	384
9%	10	865	610	277							
	15	931	801	630	489	319					
	20	961	887	791	710	614	433	197			
	25	977	933	875	827	770	662	522	404	264	
	30	986	959	924	894	859	793	707	635	549	388
9⅛%	10	865	612	278							
	15	931	802	633	491	321					
	20	961	888	793	713	617	436	198			
	25	977	934	877	830	773	666	525	407	266	
	30	986	960	925	896	862	796	711	639	553	391
9¼%	10	866	613	280							
	15	932	804	635	493	322					
	20	962	890	795	715	620	439	200			
	25	978	935	879	832	776	669	528	410	268	
	30	986	961	927	898	864	799	714	643	557	394
9⅜%	10	867	615	281							
	15	933	805	637	495	324					
	20	962	891	797	718	622	441	201			
	25	978	936	881	834	778	672	531	413	271	
	30	987	962	928	900	866	802	717	646	560	397

LOAN PROGRESS CHART

Showing the dollar balance remaining per $1000 of loan

INT RATE	ORIG TERM	ELAPSED TERM IN YEARS 2	5	8	10	12	15	18	20	22	25
9½%	10	868	616	282							
	15	934	807	639	497	326					
	20	963	893	799	720	625	444	203			
	25	978	937	883	837	781	675	535	416	273	
	30	987	962	930	902	869	805	721	650	564	400
9⅝%	10	869	618	283							
	15	934	809	641	499	328					
	20	964	894	801	723	628	446	205			
	25	979	938	885	839	784	678	538	419	275	
	30	987	963	931	904	871	808	724	653	568	404
9¾%	10	869	619	284							
	15	935	810	643	501	330					
	20	964	895	803	725	631	449	206			
	25	979	940	886	841	786	681	541	422	277	
	30	988	964	933	906	873	811	728	657	571	407
9⅞%	10	870	621	285							
	15	936	812	645	504	331					
	20	965	897	805	728	633	452	208			
	25	980	941	888	843	789	685	544	425	279	
	30	988	965	934	908	876	814	731	661	575	410
10%	10	871	622	286							
	15	936	813	647	506	333					
	20	965	898	807	730	636	454	209			
	25	980	942	890	846	792	688	547	428	282	
	30	988	966	935	909	878	817	734	664	578	413
10⅛%	10	872	623	288							
	15	937	815	649	508	335					
	20	966	899	810	733	639	457	211			
	25	980	943	892	848	794	691	551	431	284	
	30	989	967	937	911	880	819	738	668	582	416
10¼%	10	872	625	289							
	15	937	816	651	510	337					
	20	966	901	812	735	641	459	212			
	25	981	944	893	850	797	694	554	433	286	
	30	989	967	938	913	882	822	741	671	585	419
10⅜%	10	873	626	290							
	15	938	818	654	512	338					
	20	967	902	814	738	644	462	214			
	25	981	945	895	852	799	697	557	436	288	
	30	989	968	939	915	884	825	744	674	589	422
10½%	10	874	628	291							
	15	939	819	656	514	340					
	20	967	903	816	740	647	464	215			
	25	982	946	897	854	802	700	560	439	290	
	30	989	969	941	916	886	828	747	678	592	426
10⅝%	10	875	629	292							
	15	939	821	658	516	342					
	20	968	904	818	742	649	467	217			
	25	982	947	898	856	804	703	563	442	293	
	30	990	970	942	918	888	830	750	681	596	429
10¾%	10	875	631	293							
	15	940	822	660	519	344					
	20	968	906	820	745	652	470	218			
	25	982	948	900	858	807	706	566	445	295	
	30	990	970	943	919	890	833	754	685	599	432

LOAN PROGRESS CHART

Showing the dollar balance remaining per $1000 of loan

INT RATE	ORIG TERM	ELAPSED TERM IN YEARS 2	5	8	10	12	15	18	20	22	25
10⅞%	10	876	632	294							
	15	941	824	662	521	345					
	20	969	907	821	747	654	472	220			
	25	983	949	901	860	809	709	569	448	297	
	30	990	971	944	921	892	835	757	688	603	435
11%	10	877	634	296							
	15	941	825	664	523	347					
	20	969	908	823	749	657	475	221			
	25	983	950	903	862	812	712	572	451	299	
	30	990	972	945	923	894	838	760	691	606	438
11⅛%	10	878	635	297							
	15	942	827	666	525	349					
	20	970	909	825	752	660	477	223			
	25	983	950	905	864	814	714	575	454	302	
	30	991	972	947	924	896	840	763	695	610	441
11¼%	10	878	636	298							
	15	942	828	668	527	351					
	20	970	911	827	754	662	480	225			
	25	984	951	906	866	816	717	579	456	304	
	30	991	973	948	926	898	843	766	698	613	444
11⅜%	10	879	638	299							
	15	943	829	670	529	352					
	20	971	912	829	756	665	482	226			
	25	984	952	908	868	819	720	582	459	306	
	30	991	974	949	927	900	845	769	701	616	447
11½%	10	880	639	300							
	15	944	831	672	531	354					
	20	971	913	831	759	667	485	228			
	25	984	953	909	870	821	723	585	462	308	
	30	991	974	950	929	902	848	772	704	620	450
11⅝%	10	881	641	301							
	15	944	832	674	533	356					
	20	971	914	833	761	670	487	229			
	25	985	954	911	872	823	726	588	465	310	
	30	992	975	951	930	903	850	775	708	623	453
11¾%	10	881	642	302							
	15	945	834	676	535	358					
	20	972	915	835	763	672	490	231			
	25	985	955	912	874	826	729	591	468	313	
	30	992	975	952	931	905	852	777	711	626	456
11⅞%	10	882	644	304							
	15	945	835	678	537	360					
	20	972	916	837	765	675	492	232			
	25	985	956	913	876	828	731	594	471	315	
	30	992	976	953	933	907	855	780	714	630	459
12%	10	883	645	305							
	15	946	837	680	540	361					
	20	973	917	838	767	677	495	234			
	25	986	957	915	878	830	734	597	473	317	
	30	992	977	954	934	909	857	783	717	633	462
12⅛%	10	884	648	307							
	15	947	839	684	544	365					
	20	974	920	842	772	682	500	237			
	25	986	958	918	881	835	740	603	479	322	
	30	993	978	956	937	912	862	789	723	639	468

LOAN PROGRESS CHART

Showing the dollar balance remaining per $1000 of loan

INT RATE	ORIG TERM	ELAPSED TERM IN YEARS 2	5	8	10	12	15	18	20	22	25
12½%	10	886	651	309							
	15	948	842	688	548	368					
	20	974	922	845	776	687	505	240			
	25	987	960	920	885	839	745	608	485	326	
	30	993	979	958	939	915	866	794	729	646	474
12¾%	10	887	653	312							
	15	949	845	692	552	372					
	20	975	924	849	780	692	510	243			
	25	987	961	923	888	843	750	614	490	330	
	30	993	980	960	942	918	870	800	735	652	480
13%	10	888	656	314							
	15	950	847	695	556	376					
	20	976	926	852	785	697	515	246			
	25	988	963	926	891	847	755	620	496	335	
	30	994	981	962	944	922	874	805	741	658	486
13¼%	10	890	659	316							
	15	952	850	699	560	379					
	20	977	928	856	789	702	520	250			
	25	988	964	928	895	851	760	626	501	339	
	30	994	982	963	946	924	878	810	747	664	492
13½%	10	891	662	319							
	15	953	853	703	564	383					
	20	977	930	859	793	707	525	253			
	25	989	965	930	898	855	765	631	507	343	
	30	994	983	965	949	927	882	815	752	670	498
13¾%	10	892	665	321							
	15	954	855	707	568	386					
	20	978	932	862	797	711	530	256			
	25	989	967	933	901	859	770	637	512	348	
	30	995	983	967	951	930	886	820	758	676	504
14%	10	894	667	323							
	15	955	858	711	572	390					
	20	979	934	865	801	716	534	259			
	25	990	968	935	904	863	775	642	517	352	
	30	995	984	968	953	933	890	824	763	682	509
14¼%	10	895	670	326							
	15	956	860	714	576	393					
	20	980	936	868	805	720	539	262			
	25	990	969	937	907	867	780	648	523	357	
	30	995	985	970	955	935	893	829	768	688	515
14½%	10	896	673	328							
	15	957	863	718	580	397					
	20	980	937	871	809	725	544	265			
	25	991	970	939	910	870	785	653	528	361	
	30	996	986	971	957	938	897	834	774	694	520
14¾%	10	898	675	330							
	15	957	865	722	584	400					
	20	981	939	874	812	729	549	268			
	25	991	972	941	912	874	789	658	533	365	
	30	996	987	972	959	940	900	838	779	699	526
15%	10	899	678	333							
	15	958	868	725	588	404					
	20	981	941	877	816	734	554	272			
	25	991	973	943	915	877	794	664	538	369	
	30	996	987	973	960	942	903	842	784	705	532

ADDITIONAL WORKSHEETS

On the following pages are two worksheets for you to use in comparing other terms for refinancing to the calculations you already made in Chapter 6.

All the tables that appeared in Chapter 6 are repeated at the back of the book for easy reference.

WORKSHEET

FIGURING THE COSTS

Nondeductible Costs

Title Search	$________	
Title Insurance	________	
Credit Report	________	
Lawyer Fee	________	
Reappraisal Fee	________	
Loan Origination Fee	________	
Prepayment Penalty	________	
Application Fee	________	
Recording Taxes	________	
Mortgage Insurance	________	
Other Fees: ____________	________	
Total Nondeductible Fees	$________	(1)

Tax-Deductible Costs

Total Point Fee:

Loan amount (thousands)		Points charged				
______________	×	______________	× 10	=	$________	(2a)

Interest in Arrears $________ (2b)

Comparing Costs of Two Loans

Old rate: _______ New rate: _______

Loan amount (thousands): _______ Estimated annual income: _______

Interest Paid for First Two Years

Two Years' Interest on Old Loan:

Loan amount (thousands)		Interest (from Table 6.1)			
________	×	________	=	$________	(3)

Two Years' Interest on New Loan:

Loan amount		Interest			
________	×	________	=	________	(4)

Difference:

Line (3) — Line (4) $________ (5)

Monthly Payments

Monthly Payment for Old Loan:

Loan amount (thousands)		Cost per 1,000 (Table 6.2)			
________	×	________	=	$________	(6)

Monthly Payment for New Loan:

Loan amount		Cost per 1,000			
________	×	________	=	________	(7)

Difference:

Line (6) — Line (7) $________ (8)

Equity Buildup After Two Years

Two Years' Equity with Old Loan:

Loan amount (thousands)		Equity per 1,000 (Table 6.3)			
________	×	________	=	$________	(9)

Two Years' Equity with New Loan:

Loan amount		Equity per 1,000			
________	×	________	=	________	(10)

Difference:

Line (10) — Line (9) $________ (11)

COMPUTING THE BOTTOM LINE

	Column A	Column B	
Nondeductible Fees			
From line (1)		$_______	(12)
Net Deductible Fees			
Part of points deductible:			
Line (2a):			
Years of mortgage: × 2 ÷ _____			
Deductible points:		$_______	(13a)
Tax Deduction on Points			
Line (13a):			
Tax rate: ×_________			
Tax deduction:			
Net Deductible Points			
Line (2a):			
Tax deduction: −_________		$_______	(13b)
Interest in Arrears:			
Tax deduction:			
Line (2b): _________			
Tax rate: ×_________			
Tax deduction: _________			
Net Deductible Interest in Arrears:			
Line (2a): _________			
Tax deduction: _________		_______	(13c)

	Column A	Column B	
Lost Interest			
Line (12):			
Lines (13b) + (13c): ________			
Total cost:			
Total cost:			
× ________		$________	(14)
Lost Tax Benefits			
Line (5):			
Tax rate: × ________		$________	(15)
Change in Monthly Payments			
Line (8):			
× 24	$________	$________	(16)
(Positive answer in Column A; negative answer in Column B.)			
Interest Gained on Savings			
Line (16):			
× 0.091	$________	$________	(17)
(In same column as answer on line (16).)			
Gain of Equity			
From line (11)	$________		(18)

	Column A	Column B	
Total Benefits and Costs			
Total of Column A	$_______		(19)
Total of Column B		$_______	(20)
The Bottom Line			
Line (19) — Line (20)		$_______	(21)

WORKSHEET

FIGURING THE COSTS

Nondeductible Costs

Title Search	$________	
Title Insurance	________	
Credit Report	________	
Lawyer Fee	________	
Reappraisal Fee	________	
Loan Origination Fee	________	
Prepayment Penalty	________	
Application Fee	________	
Recording Taxes	________	
Mortgage Insurance	________	
Other Fees: __________	________	
Total Nondeductible Fees	$________	(1)

Tax-Deductible Costs

Total Point Fee:

Loan amount (thousands)		Points charged					
____________	×	____________	× 10	=	$________	(2a)

Interest in Arrears $________ (2b)

Comparing Costs of Two Loans

Old rate: ______ New rate: ______

Loan amount (thousands): ______ Estimated annual income: ______

Interest Paid for First Two Years

Two Years' Interest on Old Loan:

Loan amount (thousands)		Interest (from Table 6.1)			
______________	×	______________	=	$________	(3)

Two Years' Interest on New Loan:

Loan amount		Interest			
______________	×	______________	=	________	(4)

Difference:

Line (3) — Line (4)	$________	(5)

Monthly Payments

Monthly Payment for Old Loan:

Loan amount (thousands)		Cost per 1,000 (Table 6.2)			
______________	×	______________	=	$________	(6)

Monthly Payment for New Loan:

Loan amount		Cost per 1,000			
______________	×	______________	=	________	(7)

Difference:

Line (6) — Line (7)	$________	(8)

Equity Buildup After Two Years

Two Years' Equity with Old Loan:

Loan amount (thousands)		Equity per 1,000 (Table 6.3)			
______________	×	______________	=	$________	(9)

Two Years' Equity with New Loan:

Loan amount		Equity per 1,000			
______________	×	______________	=	________	(10)

Difference:

Line (10) — Line (9)	$________	(11)

COMPUTING THE BOTTOM LINE

	Column A	Column B	
Nondeductible Fees			
From line (1)		$______	(12)
Net Deductible Fees			
Part of points deductible:			
Line (2a):			
Years of mortgage: × 2 ÷ _____			
Deductible points:		$______	(13a)
Tax Deduction on Points			
Line (13a):			
Tax rate: ×________			
Tax deduction:			
Net Deductible Points			
Line (2a):			
Tax deduction: −________		$______	(13b)
Interest in Arrears:			
Tax deduction:			
Line (2b): ________			
Tax rate: ×________			
Tax deduction: ________			
Net Deductible Interest in Arrears:			
Line (2a): ________			
Tax deduction: ________		______	(13c)

	Column A	Column B	
Lost Interest			
Line (12):			
Lines (13b) + (13c): ________			
Total cost:			
Total cost:			
× ________		$________	(14)
Lost Tax Benefits			
Line (5):			
Tax rate: × ________		$________	(15)
Change in Monthly Payments			
Line (8):			
× 24	$________	$________	(16)
(Positive answer in Column A; negative answer in Column B.)			
Interest Gained on Savings			
Line (16):			
× 0.091	$________	$________	(17)
(In same column as answer on line (16).)			
Gain of Equity			
From line (11)	$________		(18)

	Column A	Column B	
Total Benefits and Costs			
Total of Column A	$________		(19)
Total of Column B		$________	(20)
The Bottom Line			
Line (19) — Line (20)		$________	(21)

TABLE 6.1 INTEREST PAID PER $1,000 AFTER TWO YEARS

Interest Rate	*15-Year Loan*	*30-Year Loan*
8.0%	$154	$159
8.5	164	169
9.0	175	179
9.5	185	189
10.0	194	199
10.5	204	209
11.0	214	219
11.5	225	229
12.0	234	239
12.5	244	249
13.0	254	260
13.5	265	269
14.0	275	279
14.5	285	290
15.0	294	300

TABLE 6.2 MONTHLY PAYMENT PER THOUSAND DOLLARS BORROWED

Interest Rate	*15-Year Loan*	*30-Year Loan*
8.0%	$9.56	$7.34
8.5	9.85	7.69
9.0	10.15	8.05
9.5	10.45	8.41
10.0	10.75	8.78
10.5	11.06	9.15
11.0	11.37	9.53
11.5	11.69	9.91
12.0	12.01	10.29
12.5	12.33	10.68
13.0	12.66	11.07
13.5	12.99	11.46
14.0	13.32	11.85
14.5	13.66	12.25
15.0	14.00	12.65

TABLE 6.3 EQUITY EARNED PER $1,000 AFTER TWO YEARS

Interest Rate	*15-Year Loan*	*30-Year Loan*
8.0%	$75	$17
8.5	72	16
9.0	69	14
9.5	66	13
10.0	64	12
10.5	61	11
11.0	59	10
11.5	56	9
12.0	54	8
12.5	52	7
13.0	50	6
13.5	47	6
14.0	45	5
14.5	43	4
15.0	42	4

TABLE 6.4 MARGINAL TAX RATES

Married Couples Filing Joint Returns		Single Persons	
Taxable Income	*Tax Rate*	*Taxable Income*	*Tax Rate*
$17,270–$21,799	.18	$13,920–$16,189	.20
21,800–26,549	.22	16,190–19,639	.23
26,550–32,269	.25	19,640–25,359	.26
32,270–37,979	.28	25,360–31,079	.30
37,980–49,419	.33	31,080–36,799	.34
49,420–64,749	.38	36,800–44,779	.38
64,750–92,369	.42	44,780–59,669	.42
92,370–118,049	.45	59,670–88,269	.48
118,050–175,249	.49	88,270+	.50
175,250+	.50		

Source: Internal Revenue Service.

ABOUT THE AUTHOR AND EDITOR

Author Don DeBat, an award-winning real estate editor, has covered the mortgage finance and housing markets for nearly two decades. He is widely known for his consumer-oriented columns which appear in the *Chicago Sun-Times*.

In 1983, DeBat's story "The Mortgage Race" won first place in the consumer category of the National Association of Real Estate Editors writing contest. The article outlined twelve ways to finance the purchase of a home.

In 1982, "The ARMs Race" pointed out the drawbacks of financing a home with an adjustable-rate mortgage, and "The Perils of Creative Finance" delved into the pitfalls of buying a home on contract with short-term balloon financing. The articles won national citations from the Real Estate Educators Association and the National Association of Real Estate Editors.

A real estate investor, DeBat has renovated and restored two vintage homes in Chicago, and he once headed a community group that won historic landmark district status for a city neighborhood. DeBat received his master's degree in 1968 and a bachelor's dregree in 1966 from the University of Missouri School of Journalism in Columbia.

Editor Thomas A. Kelly holds a master of management degree from Northwestern University's Kellogg Graduate School of Management with concentrations in finance and marketing.

His financial expertise contributed to a *Chicago Sun-Times* series inspecting private mortgage insurance. The series was first runner-up in the 1985 National Association of Real Estate Editors contest and won the 1986 feature reporting award from the Financial Institutions Marketing Assocation.

Kelly, who also holds a bachelor of science degree from Northwestern's Medill School of Journalism, is chief of the *Sun-Times* features copy desk.